# Art Deco
## SOURCE BOOK

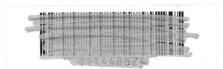

# Art Deco
## SOURCE BOOK

PATRICIA BAYER

Grange
BOOKS

A QUANTUM BOOK

Published by Grange Books
an imprint of Grange Books Plc
The Grange
Kingsnorth Industrial Estate
Hoo, nr. Rochester
Kent ME3 9ND
www.grangebooks.co.uk

1-84013-819-X

QUMADB

This book is Produced by
Quantum Publishing
6 Blundell Street
London N7 9BH

Printed in Singapore by
Star Standard Industries Pte Ltd

# AUTHOR'S NOTE

Patricia Bayer is a freelance writer, editor and consultant who has written and lectured extensively on antiquing and the decorative arts of the nineteenth and twentieth centuries. Born in Connecticut and a Manhattan resident for 14 years, she gained a Bachelor of Art degree from Barnard College, Columbia University, before completing an MA at the Institute of Fine Arts at New York University, where she also received a Certificate in Museum Training from the joint NYU/Metropolitan Museum training programme. She subsequently worked at the Metropolitan Museum of Art in New York City and later at the Virginia Museum of Fine Arts in Richmond, Virginia. From 1981–83, Ms Bayer was an associated with the New York gallery, Rosenberg & Stiebel, at which time she was also Projects Co-ordinator for the International Confederation of Art Dealers (CINOA), for whom she organized the Seventh International CINOA Exhibition.

Ms Bayer's previous books include *The Art of René Lalique* (Bloomsbury, 1988), co-authored with Mark Waller; *The Antiques World Travel Guide to America* (Doubleday/Dolphin, 1982), with Michael Goldman, and *The Fine Art of the Furniture Maker* (Memorial Art Gallery of the University of Rochester, New York, 1981). She curated *Metalworks: The Art of Albert Paley* while at the Virginia Museum in 1986. Her articles have been published in *Portfolio, Connoisseur, Art & Antiques* and *Antiques World* magazines, as well as in *London Outlook*, an American newsletter for Anglophiles.

Now living in London, Ms Bayer has been interested in Art Deco since the mid-1970s. She herself collects powder compacts and other humble but handsome objects from the period; several pieces from her collection are illustrated in this book.

ART DECO SOURCE BOOK

# CONTENTS

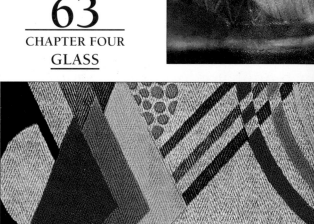

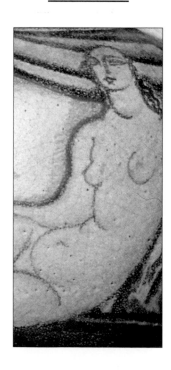

# CONTENTS

# FOREWORD

**M**y acute awareness of the Art Deco period began with a graduate-school project at New York University's Institute of Fine Arts. I was in the Museum Training Program there, a joint academic/professional effort with the Metropolitan Museum of Art, and it was at that great Manhattan institution that I met Penelope Hunter-Stiebel, who worked with the twentieth-century decorative arts collection. It was through Penelope, a vivacious, enthusiastic and highly knowledgeable expert, that I came to know and love late nineteenth- and early twentieth-century decorative arts – Art Nouveau, Arts & Crafts, but most of all Art Deco and Modernism, which heretofore I had known about in a superficial, cursory manner, and then only through rather inferior, imitation products. Penelope made me aware of the designers in 1920s Paris, men and women whose talents and creations echoed those of their great eighteenth-century counterparts, and I ended up writing a paper on a desk and chair by Süe et Mare in the Met's collection. Later, during an internship at the Museum, I came to know the works of Ruhlmann, Marinot, Dunand, Puiforcat, Lalique *et al* even better. I even came to appreciate the "beautility" of a simple chrome bud vase by Chase and a 1930s lift from New York's Rockefeller Center, both of which Penelope installed in the Twentieth-Century Decorative Arts gallery. After the Met, I worked at other museums, wrote articles and books, and lectured here and there on nineteenth- and twentieth-century decorative arts, even acquiring odd bits of Art Deco along the way.

I have come to appreciate *Le Style 25*, Modernism, the streamlined era – whatever you want to call the various and myriad manifestations, outgrowths and adaptations of Art Deco and the Machine Age – greatly over the past decade, and this book will, I trust, help others to recognize the output of the highly productive period c.1920–40. The great wealth of photographs in the book has been organized into sections which I feel best display the object, room or building's salient features – the material or techniques they are made of, the motifs with which they are adorned, their subjects, etc. The categories are of necessity subjective, but the resultant groupings are, I think, sensible, telling and appealing to look at. It was necessary, too, to divide the book's chapters according to media – such as Ceramics, Metalwork, Glass, Architecture – but as a whole, the book will doubtless give a rich overview of Art Deco which overrides categories and materials. Certain themes or motifs run through the whole period – even throughout the Western world – and one joy of the book will be to discover the international parallels, the obvious influences, if you will the aesthetic synchronism characterizing Art Deco.

Besides my mentor, Penelope Hunter-Stiebel (a fellow Barnard College and Institute of Fine Arts graduate, I might add), I would like to thank Mark Waller of Galerie Moderne, London, my co-author on *The Art of René Lalique* and supplier of many of the photographs in this book; Martine de Cervens and Isobel Baker, also of Galerie Moderne; Henrietta Wilkinson and Hazel Edington, the clever, patient editor and talented, accommodating designer of this book, respectively; Anne-Marie Ehrlich, who did such a marvellous job with the photo research; Frederick Brandt and Mary Moore Jacoby of the Virginia Museum, Diane Hart, Sheila Murphy, Andrew Stewart, Gerald Stiebel and anyone and everyone else whose expertise, encouragement, help and/or talents went into the creation of this book. Thanks most of all to Frank Murphy, for his often-tried patience and constant encouragement.

Patricia Bayer
London, March 1988

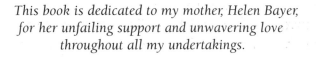

*This book is dedicated to my mother, Helen Bayer, for her unfailing support and unwavering love throughout all my undertakings.*

# INTRODUCTION

**A**rt Deco. The phrase evokes a whole spectrum of images to a great many people: opulent Parisian furnishings to purists; streamlined, minimalist designs to modernists; glittering Manhattan skyscrapers to romantics; Bakelite radios to industrial-art aficionados.

The school of luxuriant French design which reached its peak at the 1925 Paris World's Fair – the *Exposition Internationale des Arts Décoratifs et Industriels Modernes*, whence the term Art Deco is derived – is generally considered pure, high-style Art Déco (with an accent on the "e"). Over the years, however, the output of other schools and countries of the so-called Machine Age has come to be covered by the catch-all term, which, incidentally, did not begin to be used until the 1960s.

Thus, the parameters of Art Deco (generally without the accent), or *Le Style 25* as others call it, have expanded to include an extensive array of modern western architecture, design, decoration, graphics, motifs, products and even fine art dating from approximately 1915 to 1940, with the 1939–40 World's Fair in New York acting as an endpoint of sorts. Some non-French Art Deco works relate directly to Parisian design – the furniture of the German Bruno Paul or the jewellery of the American firm Black, Starr & Frost, for instance. Many other designers throughout Europe and the United States paid vestigial homage to the French style, among them the creators of the spectacular American and English motion picture palaces, the Russian-born Serge Chermayeff and the British Clarice Cliff with her jazzy, brightly hued pottery. Still others such as the Bauhaus school or the Scandinavian glassmakers created their own distinctive styles, blazing new, seemingly antithetical trails to those forged by the majority of the French.

So, far from being a school of design characterized only by geometric forms, lavishly decorated surfaces, stylized flowers, lithe female and animal figures, vivid colours and the like, as so many think of it, Art Deco is a multifaceted style for all seasons, and for all tastes.

This source book covers, through word and picture, all these and many more aspects of Art Deco, from the most pristine and precious French interiors to the glitziest and most inventive American industrial designs. In between, there are myriad wonderful objects, some documented masterpieces, others anonymous, but all undeniably, unabashedly Art Deco.

## THE SOURCES

The seeds of Art Deco were sown well before the 1925 Paris Exposition, indeed as early as the last years of the nineteenth and the first years of the twentieth centuries, when Art Nouveau still reigned supreme. This nature-inspired, essentially curvilinear and asymmetrical style experienced its zenith at the 1900 *Exposition Universelle*, which also took place in Paris, but the style's decline began soon afterwards, hastened in part by the rise of industrialization.

Sparks of modernism were set off in Vienna, where the architect-designers Otto Wagner (1841–1918), Josef Hoffmann (1870–1956) and Koloman Moser (1868–1918) started a trend towards

*Emile-Jacques Ruhlmann created the stunning armoire, left, c.1922. Veneered in exotic amaranth, the showpiece features a marquetry floral urn in ivory and Macassar ebony. Ruhlmann was influenced by French ébénisterie of the 1700s, but he subtly updated his furniture, producing twentieth-century classics.*

*The lustrous flacon, right, is by Maurice Marinot, a French painter/glassmaker who handcrafted some 2,500 pieces of blown glass. Known for their classic shapes, thick walls, and inclusions of bubbles or chemical streaks, Marinot's masterpieces influenced contemporaries as well as subsequent glass artists.*

*Outside France, Art Deco designs – such as the coffee set, above, by English ceramics designer Clarice Cliff – were often jazzy, colourful and far less restrained than their Gallic counterparts'. Cliff's vivid hues and bold patterns were in part inspired by the Ballets Russes, which had a great impact on Western designers.*

LE DÉPART POUR LE CASINO

MANTEAU DU SOIR, DE WORTH

N° 3 de la Gazette.                Modèle déposé. Reproduction interdite.                Année 1923. — Planche 1

*Colourful fashion-plates abounded in the 1920s, promoting contemporary couture as well as shaping modern illustration. On the left is George Barbier's 1923 drawing for an evening coat by Worth; it appeared in* La Gazette du Bon Ton, *an influential Parisian journal. The plate is narrative as well, depicting a chic couple bound for the casino.*

*Chryselephantine sculptures of ivory and cold-painted bronze such as the Dancer by Rumanian-born Demêtre Chiparus, above, captured the drama and exoticism of theatre and dance, the Near and Far East, and Woman herself in a sensuous manner now synonymous with Art Deco.*

rectilinearity which was to be adopted, either consciously or not, at first by French and German and later by American designers. Some of the Austrians" furniture, glass and flatware designs, even those as early as 1902, are quite modern-looking. In the same way, the Glaswegian Charles Rennie Mackintosh (1868–1928), who was much admired by the Viennese, created furniture, interiors and buildings which reflected an understated, proto-modern sensibility with their light colours, subtle curves and stark lines. They were a world apart from the uninhibited, undulating designs of his French contemporaries. Two Mackintosh clocks, for instance, both dating from 1917, are blatantly modern, rectilineal and architectonic. They even make use of Erinoid, an early synthetic made from resin or protein plastic.

Even before Mackintosh, British designers were creating mass-produced pieces with startlingly modern looks. The silver and electroplated tableware of one of the most accomplished, Christopher Dresser (1834–1904) – his pitchers, candlesticks, tureens and tea services were designed in the 1880s – is displayed today in such esteemed and decidedly contemporary collections as that of the Museum of Modern Art in New York.

The English Arts & Crafts Movement, although very much grounded in medievalist principles, practices and institutions such as the Guild, could also be said to have exerted some influence on Art Deco, albeit in a surprisingly roundabout way. The lead came chiefly from its early American exponents, who inspired later designers in the United States. Frank Lloyd Wright (1867–1959), for instance, some of whose achievements late in life were quite streamlined and Bauhaus-like, had adhered to an Arts & Crafts-type aesthetic for most of his career, even when producing mass-made furniture.

But the French designers whose works have come to exemplify Art Deco – Emile-Jacques Ruhlmann, Jean Dunand, Armand-Albert Rateau, Süe et Mare, René Lalique *et al* – were influenced less by their immediate European predecessors than by earlier periods, and even by far-off, exotic places, *if* they can be said to have been dependent on outside factors at all.

To trace the sources of Art Deco is indeed a difficult exercise. Since the style had so many often unrelated and even contradictory manifestations, its inspiration can only have been both manifold and diverse. Best known among the influences are African tribal art, Central American (Aztec and Mayan) architecture and Pharaonic Egyptian art, this last due in large part to the discovery of Tutankhamen's tomb in 1922. Influential as well were the bold designs and bright colours of the Ballets Russes, the glazes and lacquerwork of the Far East and the imagery and metalwork of classical Greece and Rome. French furniture forms of the Louis XV and Louis XVI periods also contributed and even contemporaneous fine arts such as Fauvism, Constructivism and Cubism played a part, mostly in terms of colours and shapes, especially as applied to textiles.

## THE VISIONARIES

There were, in addition, the truly modern visionaries, such as Le Corbusier (1887–1965) and his associate Charlotte Perriand (b.1903), whose functional furniture, or "equipment" as they termed it, was sharply reductionist (that is, simplified to its utmost), and is still very influential today. Interestingly, Le Corbusier's stark, all-white *Pavillon de l'Esprit Nouveau*, at the 1925 Paris Fair was in marked contrast to the ostentatious exhibits of Süe et Mare's *Compagnie des Arts Français*, Lalique, Ruhlmann, and others, yet its statement was as strongly modern – in retrospect even more so – than theirs.

The exponents of the streamlined school of the Art Deco period were primarily from America, where industrial designers such as Raymond Loewy, Walter Dorwin Teague and Walter von Nessen helped to define modern culture with their tableware, hardware, household appliances, automobiles and aircraft. Though blatantly antithetical to the Gallic school, the work of these talented Americans shaped the future in a positive, exciting way, not at all grounded in a romantic, ornamented past.

Other Americans, however, borrowed colourful, decorative elements from their French counterparts and included them in their modern architectural creations. Structures like the Chrysler and Chanin Buildings in Manhattan were latter-day temples of a kind, but devoted to industry and business, rather than to any spiritual deity. Architects throughout the United States working in their own Art Deco vein created factories, apartment complexes,

hotels and, of course, film theatres. Indeed, although Parisian architect-designers were responsible for buildings as well as for interiors and furnishings, it was their New World counterparts who excelled in these large-scale works.

The Art Deco period is renowned for its contributions in other disciplines as well as in architecture, furniture and industrial design. These include textiles and carpets, fashion, bookbinding, graphics (embracing posters, typography and advertising) and two entirely new fields in their time, lighting and cinema. Glass, ceramics, silver and other metalwork, jewellery, painting and sculpture were also treated in entirely decidedly Art Deco ways.

## REVIVALS AND REPRODUCTIONS

What of the Art Deco style today? The great objets, of course, which were produced at the height of the period's creativity are prized possessions in museums and private collections; and many of the finest buildings are being conscientiously conserved by caring enthusiasts and civic officials. Even mass-produced baubles and bric-a-brac are now sought after and saved.

Books on the subject have proliferated since the early 1970s, covering scholarly aspects of furnishings and architecture, and making designs of the day available to graphic artists. Dealers specializing in Art Deco, from kitsch ornaments to objects of museum-quality, can be found both in big cities and country towns, and antiques fairs and auctions devoted entirely to the period have sprung up as well. Tours of Art Deco architecture are

*Many Art Deco designers, French as well as British and American, were admirers of oriental lacquerwork. One of the greatest exponents of the painstaking technique was Jean Dunand, part of whose eight-panel lacquered-wood screen, Les Biches (The Does), is shown below. Made around 1931, the screen depicts a herd of grazing deer, an animal subject highly popular in the Art Déco repertory, because of their inherent beauty and elegance.*

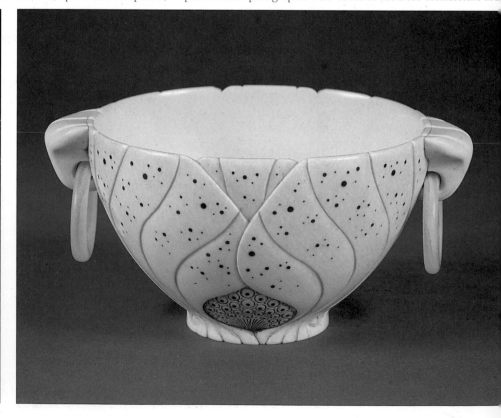

*Forged metal experienced a renaissance in 1920s France, largely due to the talents (both creative and promotional) of Edgar Brandt, whose snake-sided hammered-bronze urn is on the left. The Egyptian cobra was used by many Art Deco designers in luxuriant objets.*

*The postcard, below, advertises a Manhattan shop selling Art Deco designs. It is just one smart example of the enormous appeal of the 1920s style to collectors today*

*Parisian Art Deco creations were often noted for their use of rich, exotic materials. The vase, left, is an opulent confection of silver-inlaid ivory and onyx. It is by the Japanese Mme O'Kin Simmen, who often provided ivory or other precious touches for pieces by her husband, potter Henri Simmen, Ruhlmann and others.*

*American skyscrapers are perhaps the most exuberant manifestation of Art Deco. Right, a relief of Wisdom sits above an entrance to New York's Rockefeller Center, the massive 1930s entertainment and office complex. Lee Lawrie sculpted the panel, Leon V. Solon polychromed it, and the patterned glass blocks below are by Steuben.*

now offered in Miami Beach, New York and Tulsa, Oklahoma, and other places will no doubt follow suit.

Some of the world's top designers and craftsmen are now producing furniture and architecture with Art Deco-style embellishments, and many great pieces of the 1920s have been revived in excellent contemporary reproductions. The Italian firm Cassina, for instance, offers copies of Rietveld's famous red-and-blue chair. The Parisian interior designer Andrée Putman's Ecart International has brought out some of Eileen Gray's rugs and her *Transat* armchair, as well as Robert Mallet-Stevens" dining room chairs and a Jean-Michel Frank and A. Chanaux sofa. Chairs by Le Corbusier, Marcel Breuer and Mies van der Rohe have become design classics which continue to be produced, and even Parker has re-created a classic 1927 fountain pen, featuring it in an advertisement along with a Cassandre poster, an Eileen Gray table and a Bauhaus lamp, all again also in production. The Cristal Lalique glass firm still makes several pieces created by René Lalique in the 1920s and 1930s, and Clarice Cliff's colourful *Bizarre* ware is being manufactured again and sold in the china departments of exclusive stores.

Art Deco typefaces, graphics and colour combinations often appear in advertisements, and many stores and restaurants give prominence to Art Deco style fittings, furniture and menu designs. Contemporary films are frequently set in the 1920s and 1930s, with stunning period interiors and costumes, and interest in the original films themselves has intensified, with video cassettes readily available and revivals often taking place in 1930s picture palaces.

The following chapters will celebrate the Art Déco spirit as applied to all these media and categories, and will show why this period was one of the richest and most exciting in design history.

*Corner cabinet by Emile Jacques Ruhlmann,*
*rosewood, ivory and exotic woods,*
*France, 1916*

# CHAPTER • ONE
# FURNITURE
# AND
# INTERIORS

The elegance and opulence of Parisian Art Deco were best expressed in the stunning interiors of the 1920s and 1930s, often the products of collaboration between furniture and textile designers, sculptors, painters, lacquerworkers and numerous other talented artists and artisans. The *ensemblier* came to the fore, with such names as Emile-Jacques Ruhlmann, Robert Mallet-Stevens, Francis Jourdain, Eileen Gray, and the partnership of Louis Süe and André Mare taking on the rather formidable task of creating a total design, or ensemble, for a room, including its wall, window and floor coverings, furniture and other accessories.

Art Deco designers often paid homage to the rich heritage of the Louis XV, Louis XVI and Empire periods, as well as creating entirely new forms of their own. They used both innovative and traditional materials, although their techniques were generally subsidiary to the overall aesthetic effect. Colours were often bright and vibrant, but subtle pastel shades and deep, dark greys, browns and blacks were also in evidence. The high-style Art Deco interior and furnishings in Paris were above all luxuriant and lavish, with wealthy clients such as the couturiers Jacques Doucet, Jeanne Lanvin and Madeleine Vionnet commissioning furniture, *objets* and indeed whole rooms from the great designers.

In 1912, Jacques Doucet sold off a fine collection of eighteenth-century French furniture and Old Master paintings, and sought out instead designs by such modernists as Paul Iribe, Clément Rousseau, Rose Adler and Pierre Legrain, as well as paintings and sculpture by Picasso, Douanier Rousseau, Miró, Ernst, Brancusi and Miklos, and even pieces of the traditional Negro art, which had had a great impact on, among others, Picasso and Legrain.

Similarly, in 1920 Jeanne Lanvin commissioned Armand-Albert Rateau, known for his emulation of classical antiquity and oriental art, to design her Parisian dwelling. His patinated-bronze, wood and marble furnishings were rife with elaborate floral and animal motifs – birds supporting a bronze coffee table; deer amid foliage on a bathroom bas-relief; marguerites entwining a dressing table; firedogs in the shape of cats.

While Rateau's furniture and overall vision are among the most figurative and truly sculptural of the period – at times even whimsical – the heavily veneered, embellished and/or lacquered pieces of many of the others, are much more handsome and restrained, often deriving from classical shapes. Classical scrolls, or volutes, were also used to decorate furniture, as well as stylized wings, animals, birds and human figures. Pierre Legrain, who was influenced by African and Egyptian forms, created a wide variety of innovative furniture, from chairs of carved wood similar to those used in Tutankhamen's time to an ebony-veneered stool with a curved seat resembling a tribal stool.

Designers embellished and sometimes even entirely covered furniture with such exotic materials as mother-of-pearl, sharkskin (also known as shagreen or, in French, *galuchat*), snakeskin, gold and silver leaf, crushed-egg-shell lacquer and ivory. These might form a pattern – usually stylized flowers or a geometric motif – or they might take advantage of the nature of the substance itself,

*The dining room, above, was designed in 1924 by André Groult, the successful Parisian ensemblier whose sensitive eye and designing talent helped him create handsome, harmonious interiors. The grey, green and black palette of this room nicely complements the painting over the sideboard, which depicts a fashionable couple fishing; it could very well represent a pastel-hued canvas by Marie Laurençin, to whom Groult was related.*

*The exotic bronze chair, right, was concocted by Armand-Albert Rateau, one of France's most original – if somewhat eccentric – designers. But for its leopard skin cushion, it is awash with marine motifs – scallop shells at the top and along the back, and tentacle-like legs. Rateau's best-known commission was to fit out the Paris home of Jeanne Lanvin.*

*...ussian-born architect/designer Serge ...hermayeff was educated and ...orked in Britain, settling in the US ...1939. The walnut- and* *coromandel-veneered sideboard, below, was part of a handsome dining room he designed when working for British furniture makers Waring & Gillow.*

...erhaps using the imbrication pattern of the shark's skin decora-...vely. The shapes of furniture ranged from overtly traditional – ...ghteenth-century bureau plats, petite ladies' desks, gondole or ...rgère chairs – to the strikingly *moderne*, severely rectilinear with ...t a curve in sight.

The greatest *ébéniste*, or cabinet-maker, of Art Deco France, ...mile-Jacques Fuhlmann (1879–1933), produced forms both ...mple and elegant, usually traditional in shape and technique, but ...eekly modern in decoration and detail. His desks, cabinets, tables ...d chairs were veneered in costly, warm woods, such as ...maranth, amboyna, ebony and violet wood, and embellished with ...k tassels and subtle touches of ivory in dentate, dotted or ...amond patterns. The long, slender legs sometimes torpedo-...aped with cut facets – were often capped with metal sabots, or ...oes, a concept that was both decorative and practical. He even ...ed chrome and silvered metal towards the end of his career, ...hen many of his furniture forms became quite rectilinear; at the ...me time, his ivory dots and silk fringes gave way to chrome ...tings, leather cushions and swivel bases. Ruhlmann was also the ...preme *ensemblier*, designing rugs, fabrics, wallpaper and porce-...n; in this guise he triumphed at the 1925 Paris Exposition with ...s *Hôtel d'un collectionneur* – the imagined town house of a wealthy ...nnoisseur. He was a fine draughtsman as well, and in 1924 he ...blished a book containing water colours of his interiors and ...tailed studies of sketches which followed the stages of his design ...om initial idea to finished product.

Jean Dunand (1877–1942), known for his *dinanderie* (the art of

chasing and hammering metal) and for his lacquerwork, also designed and decorated elaborate furniture, including cabinets, panels and screens. These were often covered with figural or animal designs, either by Dunand himself or after a noted artist. The pieces themselves may have been designed by an *ébéniste*. An especially stunning black-lacquer cabinet in the 1925 Exposition, for instance, was designed by Ruhlmann and lacquered by Dunand with a charming scene of two fantastic animal-hybrids after a pictorial composition by Jean Lambert-Rucki. His huge screens, often of silver, gold and black lacquer, displayed massive geometric motifs, exotic oriental or African maidens, lush landscapes or elaborate mythological scenes. Among these last is a pair made of lacquered wood, designed by Séraphin Soudbinine for the Long Island, New York, home of Mr and Mrs Solomon R. Guggenheim, and depicting the *Battle of the Angels: Crescendo* and *Pianissimo*. They are now in the Metropolitan Museum of Art, New York.

Irish-born Eileen Gray (1879–1933), another great Parisian furniture designer and *ensemblier*, started out fashioning exquisite handmade objects such as screens, tables and chairs. These were often embellished with Japanese lacquer, whose technique she studied with the master Sougawara. Eventually she moved on to more rectilinear and strongly functional furniture, as well as to architecture. For modiste Suzanne Talbot (Mme Mathieu Lévy) she designed a Paris apartment in 1919–20 which included a canoe-shaped chaise-longue in patinated bronze lacquer with subtle scalloped edges and a base comprising 12 rounded arches. By 1927, however, her chair designs were radically different and

*The Parisian interior decorating firm, the Compagnie des Arts Français, founded by Louis Süe and André Mare, Created the stunning cabinet, above, in 1927. Veneered in Macassar ebony and featuring a marquetry floral bouquet of mother-of-pearl and abalone, the showpiece was part of the furnishings designed for the Saint-Cloud villa of French actress Jane Renouardt. The wing-like feet and leafy gallery are elements of eighteenth-century-French furniture updated and streamlined by Süe et Mare; in the Louis XV period, however, they would have been gilt-bronze, not carved wood.*

distinctly *moderne*. A padded-leather-seat *Transat* armchair, set on a rigid lacquer frame with chromed-steel connecting elements, was more akin to Le Corbusier than to Ruhlmann, Dunand *et al.* Her case pieces, with built-in cupboards that featured swivelling drawers and doors set on tracks, and tables that moved easily on wheels, were even more practical.

Le Corbusier's best-known furniture pieces are his chairs, designed in collaboration with his cousin Pierre Jeanneret and Charlotte Perriand. His chaise-longues and armchairs, often fashioned of tubular-steel frames and simple but comfortable and functional leather seats, were slightly more inviting than the spare, minimal designs of the Bauhaus school. These, especially the designs of Marcel Breuer and Mies van der Rohe, were even further removed from the plush, upholstered chairs of André Groult, Maurice Dufrêne and Dominique, all of which recalled a luxuriant past. Theirs instead clearly signalled a new era in design which still reigns today.

In between the elegantly carved and veneered confections of high-style Parisian Art Deco and the near-antithetical, ultra-*moderne* tubular-steel and leather creations of Le Corbusier and the others were myriad pieces of furniture by Europeans and Americans that reflected either – at times even both – of the Art Deco design schools, with the occasional completely innovative design making its own waves.

In Great Britain, which had its strong native tradition of solid Arts & Crafts-style furniture, craftsmen such as Edward Barnsley

designed sturdy, rectilinear pieces that bore no reflection whatsoever of moderne continental designs. Others, however, such as Betty Joel, Ambrose Heal, Russian-born Serge Chermayeff, Gordon Russell and the design firm PEL (Practical Equipment Limited) produced functionalist furniture with distinctly modern lines and, especially in the case of Chermayeff, occasional stylized-floral designs.

Quite apart from the Bauhaus designers was a group of Germans who created furniture more in the elaborate Parisian mode. Bruno Paul, an architect-designer, was one such who successfully catered to an elite bourgeois clientele in the 1920s and 1930s. As Ruhlmann and Süe et Mare distilled classic eighteenth-century French furniture design, so Paul attempted to update the German Baroque tradition. His veneered pieces were often embellished with ivory knobs and finials, à la Ruhlmann, but his forms were more awkward and less sleek than those of the French, the legs more serpentine than gently tapering.

In Holland, De Stijl architect-designer Gerrit Rietveld created his famous *Rood Blauwe Stoel* (red-and-blue chair) in 1918. Just as the De Stijl movement's painters in Holland combined simple geometric shapes, primary colours and horizontal and vertical lines in their canvases, so this classic chair ably combined these same ingredients in a three-dimensional manner; the final result may have been uncomfortable, but it has none the less become an icon of modern design.

In the United States, furniture ran the gamut from variations on

*The wood, glass and tubular metal table, below, is by Eileen Gray, the Irish-born French-based designer whose far-seeing furniture, object and building designs were distinctive moderne exercises. Some pieces are opulent, extravagant, even whimsical confections (see pages 26 and 101), but most of the later designs, like the table pictured, are practical and elegant modern classics.*

*A simple side table has been transformed into a precious piece of furniture, right, by the talented Jean Dunand. Redlacquer squares embellish the delicate table – which is lacquered all over in black – but its salient features is the mass of coquille d'oeuf (crushed eggshell) covering the top surface. Dunand learned the difficult, time-consuming art of lacquering from the Japanese master Sougawara, afterward producing masterpieces of jewellery, bookbinding, metalwork and furniture which used lacquers of all types.*

*Betty Joel was an English furniture designer who, with her husband David, founded her eponymously named firm around 1919. The chaise longue, left, was one of the more elegant furniture pieces designed by Betty Joel. Her output tended to be smoothly curved, casual and functional, although she often used exotic wood veneers. Designing good-looking and easy-to-take-care-of furniture and interiors for contemporary working women was a particular concern of Betty Joel.*

steel frames enamelled in a warm russet-brown tone which complements the American walnut of the chair arms and desk top, as well as the chair's brown-toned upholstery. The two pieces are an essay on the circle, oval and line – and undoubtedly far more inviting to an office worker than, for example, the shiny chrome-and-black-leather pieces of Breuer *et al.*

Eliel Saarinen, Eugene Schoen, Wolfgang Hoffmann (son of the Viennese Josef Hoffmann and an American emigrant), Gilbert Rohde and Joseph Urban were among the many designers who applied their talents to creating furniture for the American market. On the whole, their pieces were sturdy, mass-produced and distinctly modernist, some with echoes of French, German and Viennese design, others uniquely American in their form, colour and materials. Aluminium, chromium and other metal furniture was in the ascendancy, but wooden pieces continued to thrive, with veneers of native woods such as holly, birch, burr maple and walnut handsomely covering large surface areas. Such synthetic materials as Formica and Lucite were already being used in furniture design, with an armchair by Elsie de Wolfe, its traditional scrolled-back design of moulded Lucite, demonstrating a strange but witty meeting of the old and the new.

Metal-furniture companies and studios included the Herman Miller Furniture Co in Michigan, Warren McArthur, Kantack & Co and Deskey-Vollmer, all in New York. The large wood furniture makers included Heywood-Wakefield in Boston, plus a clutch of companies in Grand Rapids, Michigan, foremost among them the Johnson-Handley-Johnson Co. At the far end of the spectrum was T. H. Robsjohn-Gibbings, in California, working in a luxurious, fiercely anachronistic neo-classical style which greatly appealed to wealthy clients in the show-business community. Classical motifs such as scrolls, palmettes, lyres, rams" heads and hoof feet adorned his tables, mirrors and chairs, mostly made of parcel-gilt carved wood and gilt-bronze.

*The lacquered wood and mother-of-pearl table and chairs, above, were designed around 1921 by Viennese-born Joseph Urban. Urban's domestic furniture often reflected his theatrical bent (he was once a designer for the Ziegfeld Follies and the Metropolitan Opera), these three lavish pieces included. Urban was the head of the short-lived (1922–24) Wiener Werkstätte in Manhattan.*

both the high-style French and functionalist Le Corbusier schools to sized-down architectonic essays and blatant neo-classical designs. Paul Frankl, whose 1930 cry, "Ornament = crime", was taken up by a good many moderne American designers, created distinctive skyscraper bookcases and cabinets, with stepped sections and intricate compartments. Kem Weber and J. B. Peters, two Los Angeles designers, also adapted the skyscraper style to their tall pieces, and Chicagoan Abel Faidy produced a leather settee with a whimsical design derived from architecture for a private penthouse apartment which could easily have been custom-built for Radio City or the Chrysler Building.

The metal and wood furniture of Frank Lloyd Wright was not as severe as that of the Bauhaus school. For instance, his renowned 1936–39 desk and chair, called *Cherokee Red* and designed for the S. C. Johnson & Son building in Racine, Wisconsin, have their

## JACQUES DOUCET

Besides being one of the greatest couturiers in early twentieth-century France, Jacques Doucet (1853–1932) was also one of the premier collectors of fine and decorative art of the period. Doucet had accumulated a renowned collection of Old Master paintings and eighteenth-century French furniture when, in 1912, he decided to auction it off and furnish his Paris flat with later paintings, sculpture and contemporary furnishings.

At first he championed the works of Degas, Monet, Manet and other modern painters, but later he began to purchase more avant-garde work –

Braques, Picassos, Modiglianis, Mir¢s, Ernsts and Brancusis – featuring them, along with another of his loves, African art, in rooms designed by and/or containing *objets* by the likes of Paul Iribe, Pierre Legrain, Rose Adler, Eileen Gray, AndrE Groult and other great names of French Art Deco.

The room pictured was part of his studio at Neuilly, whose interior decoration was overseen by Pierre Legrain around 1925. The sofa, by Marcel Coard, is of rosewood, ivory and leather (the wood has been carved to resemble rattan); hanging over the sofa is Henri Rousseau's painting, *The Snake Charmer.*

*Pierre Chareau designed the library, below, for the 1925 Paris Exposition; it was featured in the Ambassade Française. Chareau was an* architect/interior decorator born into a family of shipbuilders. His love of fine woods is evident in this elegant room.

*The dining room, left, which was displayed at the 1925 Paris Exposition, was conceived by R. Quibel. The furniture wood is palissander; glass and silver by René Lalique and Jean Puiforcat, respectively, were also part of the entire ensemble.*

*Vivid yellow tones enliven this smoking room designed by Francis Jourdain, a painter/printmaker/ designer whose creations ranged from fabrics to aeroplanes. The water- colour, too, is by Jourdain, whose father, Frantz, was first president of the Salon d'Automne.*

The young man's bedroom, left, by M. Guillemard, was furnished by Primavera, the atelier connected to the Parisian department store, Au Printemps. Note the built-in bed, the centre table with wrought-iron base and the geometric designs on the carpet, echoed throughout the decidedly masculine room.

Master ensemblier Emile-Jacques Ruhlmann created the young girl's room, above, which was included in Jean Badovici's Intérieurs Français in 1925. Ruhlmann expertly designed all the facets of this room, as he did those of so many others. In this case he has created an elegant feminine space, with furniture veneered in warm woods, wall-covering with a charming fountain and tree design, and earthy toned floor and upholstery coverings, which are prettily offset by the bright floral paintings on the walls.

The interior decorator André Groult designed the living room, above, which was published in Jean Badovici's Intérieurs Français, 1925. Groult was married to fashion designer Paul Poiret's sister, Nicole, and designed fabrics for her firm. He also worked with his relative Marie Laurencin.

The bright and capacious bathroom, right, was designed by Marcel Dalmas and featured at the 1925 Paris Exposition. The octagonal window over the tub nicely complements the mirror surmounting the console table on the right.

# GEOMETRIC

The two chests of drawers on the right were designed by Paul T. Frankl, who studied architecture and engineering in Europe and became a significant figure in American design in the 1920s and 30s. Made of ebony-trimmed walnut (with green-lacquered interiors), the c.1928 case pieces are fine examples of his skyscraper designs, architectonic pieces intended to feel at home in high-rise urban apartments – and to provide a maximum of storage space as well. Besides designing furniture, Viennese-born Frankl (who went to the United States in 1914) was also an influential writer, and author of two important books, New Dimensions (1928) and Form and Re-form (1930), both of which featured photographs by Frankl of his works.

The dining table and chairs, left, are of glass and chromed metal, with the table featuring inlaid panels by René Lalique. The handsome set was from Asprey & Co, the London firm best known for its jewellery. Note the columnar base and feet on the table, architectural references fitted with lighting.

The Finnish architect/designer Alvar Aalto created the chair and blocky sideboard, left. Bent laminated wood, like that of the chair, was often employed by Aalto, who in 1931 founded Artek, a Helsinki firm which made furniture, lighting fixtures and fabrics.

The great American architect Frank Lloyd Wright designed the oak side chair, above, for the Imperial Hotel in Tokyo. The c.1916–22 chair is an essay in geometry – all angles and no curves. Like many of his creations, the chair is attractive but not very comfortable.

Gerrit Rietveld's Rood Blauwe Stoel (Red and Blue Chair) of 1918, left, has become an icon of modern design, its simple lines and bright colour blocks reflecting the works of the De Stijl painters in Rietveld's native Holland.

The great Art Deco furniture designer and ensemblier, Emile-Jacques Ruhlmann, created the elegant chiffonier, below, around 1926. Veneered in amboyna wood, the piece features brass hardware and ivory highlights. The geometric pattern on

the front is inlaid ivory, and a line of ivory trails down the front sides of the piece, gently tapering from a scroll at the top to a hairline at the capped foot.

The suite of living room furniture, above, was designed by Félix Del Marle in 1926 for a certain "Madame B" in Dresden. The French painter Del Marle was a Futurist converted to Cubism and then to the forms of the Dutch De Stijl movement, the latter of which were applied to this geometric suite of painted wood and metal and frosted glass. Mondrian was an admirer of Del Marle's furniture.

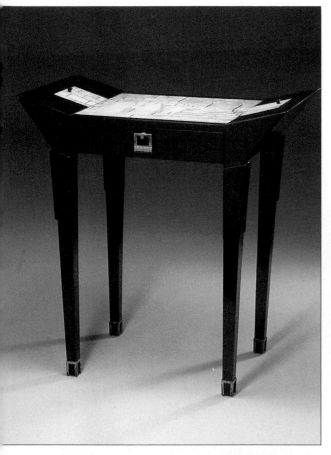

Around 1926 Rose Adler designed the table, left, of ebony, sharkskin, metal and enamel, for couturier Jacques Doucet, in whose studio it was topped by Gustave Miklos's rock-crystal sculpture (see page 156). Adler also designed bookbindings for Doucet (see page 179). The sharkskin top sports a design of stairways and stepped buildings.

The bookcase, below, with its maze-like motifs, is the result of a c.1927–28 collaboration between Eugäne Printz and Jean Dunand. The doors are copper inlaid with silver, and all seven are mounted on pivots which revolve to reveal sycamore-lined shelves. The exterior is of palmwood.

The red-lacquered "puzzle" desk by Paul T. Frankl, below, is embellished with silver-leafed drawers and silvered-metal handles. The ingenious, compartmentalized design is part whimsy and part homage to oriental forms and techniques, which fascinated Frankl on a trip to Japan at the start of his long career. Frankl opened a gallery in Manhattan in 1922, which sold his own furniture, imported wallpapers and fabrics.

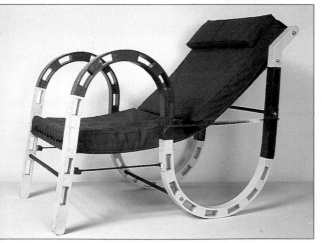

The wood and canvas armchair, above, dates from c.1938 and was designed by the versatile Eileen Gray. The serpentine line of the openwork painted-wood frame differs considerably from the rigid lacquered frame of her famous Transat chair of 1927 (see page 35), yet the basic shapes of the two are the same.

# MATERIALS

The pirogue (canoe) sofa, below, was designed c.1919–20 by Irish-born Eileen Gray. Possibly influenced by watercraft of the South Seas, the sumptuous sofa is both lacquered and silver-leafed. Gray studied the art of lacquerwork with the Japanese master Sougawara.

A tense jungle confrontation between a snake and panther is depicted in lacquer and ivory on the screen, right, executed by Jean Dunand from a design by Paul Jouve. Better known as a book illustrator, Jouve was fascinated with wild beasts, especially the cat family.

The two chairs, left, are by Clément Rousseau. Their frames are rosewood, their predominant material sharkskin (shagreen), with floral designs on the tops and sunbursts on the aprons.

Sir Edward Maufe designed the desk, right, for the 1925 Paris Fair. Its boxy shape echoed Arts & Crafts designs, but its materials – camphor, mahogany, ebony gessoed and gilded with white gold – were opulent enough to rival the greatest French pieces.

Elsie de Wolfe, one of New York's premier interior designers in the 1930s, created the side chair, below, for Hope Hampton, c.1939. Its scallop back is reminiscent of German Biedermeier furniture, but what makes the chair so astonishing is its out-of-the-ordinary use of Lucite – a durable acrylic plastic made by the E. I. du Pont de Nemours firm – for the "traditional" back and legs.

The c.1925–27 desk, right, by Emile-Jacques Ruhlmann, is an opulent piece of furniture veneered in Macassar ebony and embellished with snakeskin, ivory and silvered bronze, the latter a handsome and protective device "capping" the feet. Although marked by subtle curves, the desk has many angular elements, presaging Ruhlmann's later chrome-mounted, largely geometric pieces.

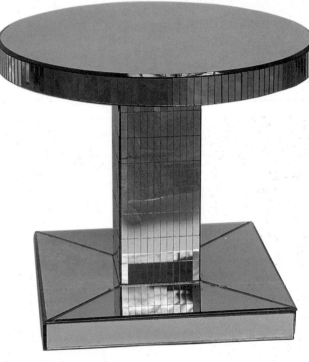

The smart coffee table, above, shimmers with peach-coloured glass. Made in the United Kingdom c.1930, the mirror-veneered table has a carcass (or frame) of wood. Such showy white- or coloured-glass-covered furniture often featured in public and private rooms in the 1930s. Blue glass was especially popular in the United States, where it even embellished a streamlined Sparton radio design of 1936 by Walter Dorwin Teague.

Emile-Jacques Ruhlmann was known for his use of exotic woods and inlays, and the Macassar ebony-veneered mirror and armchair, left, both of which are attributed to the Parisian master, are no exceptions. The mirror frame is embellished with ivory.

Since first admiring oriental lacquerwork, Jean Dunand determined to learn the painstaking procedures involved with the art. The lovely red-lacquer table, below, with its chequerboard pattern in coquille d'oeuf (crushed eggshell) is proof positive of his mastery of the technique.

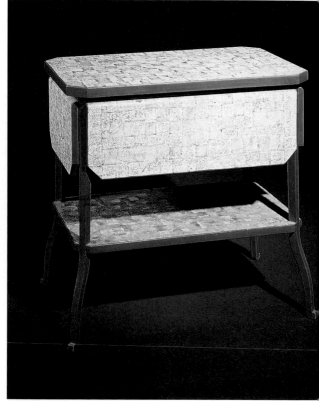

Pierre Legrain and Jean Dunand collaborated on the red-lacquered cabinet, far left Commissioned by fashion designer Jacques Doucet, its doors open to reveal 24 file drawers lacquered in a red slightly lighter than on the outside. The detail, left, shows the pivoting pewter lock which closes the two doors; it has a stylized floral design.

…he chaise-longue, below, was …signed by Pierre Legrain c.1925 …nd was very much influenced by …ibal African forms. It is of …eechwood and black lacquer and …atures mother-of-pearl inlay and …cotic zebra skin upholstery.

Viennese-born Paul T. Frankl, who emigrated to the United States in 1914, designed the man's cabinet and mirror, right, c.1938. Red and black lacquered wood comprise the cabinet, with half moons of silver- and gold-plated metal enhancing its doors. Silver leaf was applied to the top, gold leaf to the bottom.

…alissander-wood veneer and an …ched-glass top comprise the elegant …rfaces of the table, above, by Pierre …hareau. Dating from c.1928, the

table has a simple pedestal form. Note the horizontal and vertical directions of the veneer.

American designer Paul T. Frankl's Chinese-style chairs, right, are a pair from a set of 14. The lacquered chairs were inspired in part by Frankl's visit to the Orient early in his career. Many of his pieces were lacquered in red and black and embellished with gold leaf, whether derived from the East or created in a more moderne vein. Viennese-born Frankl opened up a gallery in New York City in 1922.

The Macassar ebony, marquetry, gilt-wood and marble commode, above, is a stunning creation of the Compagnie des Arts Français, the Paris design firm established by Louis Süe and André Mare. Depicted in colourful pieces of exotic wood on the front is a rich underwater scene, decorated to a Mathurin Méheut design. The massive feet of the commode, which is an updated eighteenth-century French piece, echo the shapes of the tortoises" shells on the marquetry panel.

Paul Follot, a designer for Au Bon Marché's Pomone atelier, created the rounded display cabinet, right, in dark wood and ivory, with a floral motif carved on the vertical side panel. It was exhibited at the 1925 Paris Exposition.

Above is a group of two rosewood bergère armchairs and two matching boudoir chairs, in the style of Paul Follot (see tall cabinet on opposite page). Besides the carved wood floral swags at the top, carved tassels embellish the chairs, a clever recreation in wood of the silken fringes so popular in Art Deco Paris.

The massive palissander-veneered bar, right, is inlaid with mother-of-pearl and various stained woods. It is attributed to Jules Leleu, whose pieces were often decorated with all-over designs of tiny florets and leaves.

The above silvered-bronze medallion features on an amboyna-wood-veneered cabinet by Emile-Jacques Ruhlmann. The medal, featuring a tiptoeing female nude, was made by Foucault, with whom the master Ebéniste often collaborated.

Clément Rousseau designed the stunning chair, right, of ebony, ivory and sharkskin. Signed and dated 1921, the back of the chair features a stylized sunburst design, a motif highly popular in the Art Deco period, on everything from luxuriant furniture such as this, to stained glass windows and mass-produced biscuit tins.

Exotic scenes inspired by the flora and fauna of Africa were found on many objects in the Art Deco era. Above, a four-panel screen by Jean Dunand, featuring a trio of playful monkeys amid lush tropical flowers and vegetation.

The bedroom suite, below, by Britain's Omega Workshops dates from early 1912–18 and is quite removed from the opulent materials, techniques and taste of French Art Deco. The furniture, however, does feature stylized flowers and leaves not unlike those on the screen by Jean Dunand on the top right hand side of the page.

The bureau plat by Clément Mère, below, is decorated with elements of the Parisian designer's characteristic tooled and lacquered leather. Here the drawers are "veneered" with a stylized floral motif in repoussé leather. The round knobs are in galuchat (sharkskin).

The pair of plush bergère armchairs, below, ere upholstered with Aubusson tapestry after a floral design by Paul Véra, who also worked for the Beauvais factory. Many top designers in France worked with fabric and upholstery firms, translating to textiles their decorative motifs. Tapestry design experienced a renaissance in the Art Deco period, largely due to the talents of painter-turned-designer Jean Lurçat.

he petite commode by Paul Iribe, ove, dates to 1912 and was part of e furnishings couturier Jacques oucet commissioned for his avenue Bois apartment. The basic wood is ahogany, the carved swags are ony, the "veneer" is dyed-green arkskin and on top is a slab of ack marble. The delicate form hoes eighteenth-century French rniture, but the materials and otifs are quite moderne.

e gilt and lacquered carved wood nel, right, is attributed to Paul ra. Depicted on her snorting steed a sleek, black-lacquered goddess ana, her bow taut and hair flowing. e background is of geometric and fy forms.

Right, a vintage photograph of the "Great Workroom" of the S. C. Johnson Building, Racine, Wisconsin, designed and furnished by Frank Lloyd Wright in the late 1930s. The smart desk and chair sets, an example of which is seen below, are of enamelled-steel, walnut, brass-plated metal and upholstery. Like the circular exterior of the building, the furniture comprises circles, ovals and arcs.

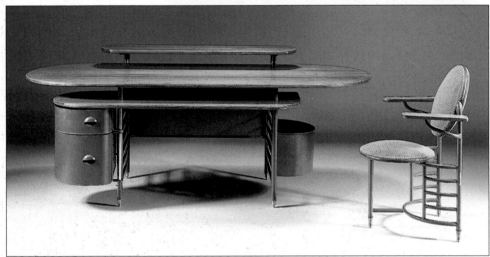

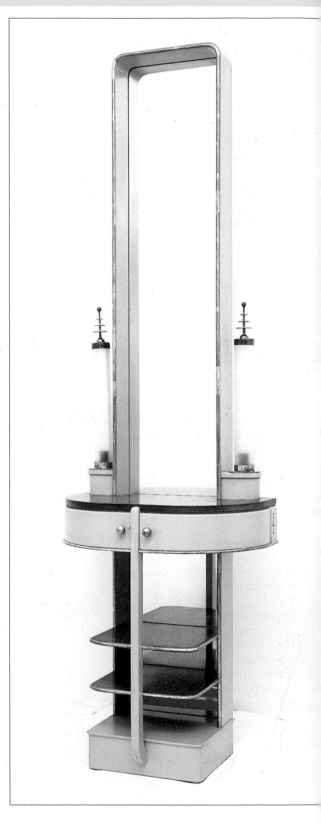

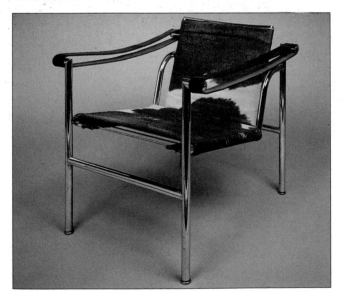

California-based Kem Weber designed the side table, right, for a San Franciscan couple, the Bissingers. Made of burl walnut, glass, silvered and painted wood, chromium-plated metal, maple and cedar, the piece is crisp and architectonic (especially its skyscraper-like sidelights).

Timeless metal furniture was designed by Le Corbusier and his associates Pierre Jeanneret and Charlotte Perriand; left, their 1928 armchair with chromium-plated steel tubing.

*Donald Deskey, responsible for the interior decoration of Radio City Music Hall in the New York, designed the executive suite for S. L. Rothafel, left, furnishing it with desk, chair and lamps of chrome-plated steel and tubular aluminium.*

*Eileen Gray made frequent use of metal in her designs, including her lacquered Transat (short for Transatlantique) chair with chromed-steel connectors and a small side table, both seen below.*

## ARMAND-ALBERT RATEAU

Some of the most original – not to mention whimsical – furniture being produced in Art Deco Paris was designed by Armand-Albert Rateau (1882–1938), who studied at the Ecole Boulle and then managed the Maison Alavoine decorating workshops from 1905–14. His largely patinated-bronze and solid-oak pieces, often inspired by furniture and other objects seen on a trip to Herculaneum and Pompeii, were very much in vogue in 1920s Paris.

The fashion designer Jeanne Lanvin commissioned him to design her entire rue Barbey-de-Jouy, Paris, town-house (finished in 1922); shown is a period photograph of Mme Lanvin's bedroom, which featured blue silk wall-coverings shot with golden threads, a built-in sleeping chamber, and bronze dressing table, standard lamp and low table (see colour photo of similar table, right); the room has been recreated at the Musée des Arts Décoratifs in Paris. Another piece made for Mme Lanvin was a patinated-bronze chaise-longue, supported by four does and with an openwork surface.

*Armand-Albert Rateau designed the patinated-bronze and marble table, above, c.1924. A similar low table was featured in the apartment of couturière Jeanne Lanvin, who commissioned Rateau to decorate and furnish her Paris residence in 1920 (see box, left). Like this piece, with its avian ball-and-claw feet, much of Rateau's work showed his admiration of oriental art and classical antiquity.*

*Silver-plated footed bowl by Gérard Sandoz, France, 1925*

# CHAPTER • TWO
# METALWORK
# AND
# SILVER

# METALWORK AND SILVER

Art Deco metalwork is dominated by Parisian design, notably by Edgar Brandt, Jean Dunand and Jean Puiforcat. They worked in three entirely different manners, however, each producing distinctive metalwork which inspired designers in France, the rest of Europe and the United States.

Edgar Brandt (1880–1960) was an ironworker of immense talent and breadth who created jewellery, vases, lamps and firedogs, as well as grilles, doors, panels and screens. He often collaborated with architects and glass-makers, as at the 1925 Paris Exposition, where his several successful exhibits gained him worldwide recognition. His designs – also executed in copper, bronze, gold and silver – often combined animal and human forms with floral and/or geometric patterns. Many of his surfaces were hammered in a decorative manner, as that of a lovely bronze platter which featured seaweed and other marine motifs. His cobra standard lamp, the coiling serpent acting as foot, stem and holder for its Daum glass shade, is one of his most striking creations. He also made small andirons in the shape of cobras and jardinières with cobra handles. The snake, taken from Egyptian art, was a popular Art Deco subject also used by Jean Dunand, René Lalique, François-Emile Décorchement and others.

Brandt's most popular designs by far featured attractive human and animal forms, usually in openwork floral or foliated surrounds. One fireplace screen (sold in France as well as America, through Ferrobrandt, the artist's New York outlet) depicted a deer in an asymmetrical setting, and is reminiscent of designs by Dagobert Peche for the Wiener Werkstätte. A pair of gates in the Virginia Museum, Richmond, dating from about 1929, is more abstract, with two central medallions of female heads surrounded by rigid tendrils, while two massive doors he produced for Ruhlmann's pavilion at the 1925 Exposition featured eight slender nudes frolicking in leafy panels.

Other French metalworkers included Raymond Subes, Paul Kiss, Armand-Albert Rateau (whose work is treated in the furniture section), Louis Sognot and Nic Frères. Their console tables, lighting fixtures, grilles, doors and screens were beautifully executed and featured various motifs from the Art Deco repertory, but in the end it was Brandt's oeuvre which set the standard not only for French but for other European and American ironwork as well.

Jean Dunand (1877–1942) was a designer *extraordinaire* who trained first as a sculptor. He directed his talents to various mediums, but finally made his name as a lacque worker, applying the coloured resin to wood and metal surfaces and creating jewellery, bookbindings, vases, tables, panels, screens and mantelpieces of the utmost beauty. (His furniture is discussed in that section.) Initially Dunand practised *dinanderie*, the art of hammering and chasing metal – copper, pewter, silver and steel – often decorating the pieces with organic motifs. In the early 1900s, however, he became

enamoured of Far Eastern art, especially admiring the lacquerwork on oriental metal vases. He studied the difficult craft with Japanese masters, notably the Paris-based Sougawara, and thereafter devoted his career to it. He collaborated with various artists, sculptors and furniture designers, even with couturiers, on whose fabrics and accessories he painted geometric designs with lacquer.

But the vases which Dunand created singlehandedly stand as his most significant contributions to the Art Deco style. Of traditional oriental shapes – mostly ovoid and spherical – these vessels were transformed into *chefs d'oeuvre* by means of his application of coloured lacquer, often in bold zigzags, triangles or streaks of black, red or gold. He even encrusted tiny bits of eggshell – *coquille d'oeuf* – into the lacquer, another eastern technique whose application he widely expanded by creating lovely geometric patterns with the fragments. Several Cubist-inspired vases sported applied wings or ellipses, often off-balance, which were lacquered in contrasting shades to the solid-coloured bodies. Dunand also designed jewellery –

*The 1927–28 lift door, below, once adorned Selfridge's in London. The Parisian metal-worker Edgar Brandt designed the wrought-iron and bronze panel, which features an octagonal medallion of exotic birds in a surround of stylized sunrays and volutes.*

bracelets, earrings and brooches – in strong geometric shapes, usually highlighted with red, black and gold lacquer. In much of his design, he took his inspiration from Africa.

Jean Puiforcat (1897–1945) also worked in metal, and his stunning creations in silver and silver-gilt, often with semi-precious stone and glass embellishments, occupy a unique place in Art Deco design. He was born into a family of goldsmiths, beginning as an apprentice in their workshop and later studying sculpture. He first exhibited in 1922, and as the years went on his designs became pure geometric statements, devoid of nearly all decoration. He worked with silver in an attempt to attain a Platonic ideal of form through mathemetical harmony and geometry.

His 1920s tea sets, dishes and bowls, which often included ivory finials, jade handles and the like, gave way by 1930 to purer, sleeker shapes – bold statements of form and volume with only the occasional touch of ice-green or salmon-pink glass, wood or crystal. Puiforcat's later works, amongst them silver *objets* for the liner *Normandie*, could also appear futuristic – a covered candy dish resembling a shiny UFO, for instance, or a cylindrical vase with a crenellated relief design.

Georg Jensen (1866–1935), although he was a Dane and worked in his native land, exerted much influence on Parisian Art Deco, as he had previously done on Art Nouveau. Not only were his wares shown to great acclaim at the 1925 Paris Exposition, but he was also admired and imitated by artists of the calibre of Puiforcat. He opened shops in Paris in 1919, London in 1920 and New York in 1923, the last having a marked influence on silver design in America. He himself often hand-worked his elegant and refined vessels – with hammered and chased surfaces and such decorative details as silver beads, leaves and openwork stems.

Jean Goulden (1878–1947) created clocks, lamps, boxes and other *objets* in metal, often embellished with coloured enamelling, a process he learned from Dunand, with whom he sometimes collaborated. His avant-garde, highly angular works often resembled Cubist and Constructivist sculpture. Camille Fauré (1872–1956) also worked with enamel on metal, but, unlike Goulden's pieces, Fauré's vessels were dominated by the coloured enamel, sometimes in stylized-floral designs, but more often in geometric configurations in the style of abstract paintings. He worked in Limoges for over 50 years.

There were also various Art Deco medallists working in silver, bronze and other metals, not only in France, but in England, Germany and the United States. The Hungarian-born Tony Szirmai, who was based in Paris, specialized in commemorative pieces. Pierre Turin produced bronze, copper and silvered-metal plaques, often octagonal, which featured stylized figures and flowers. André Lavrillier created a handsome medal depicting Leda and the Swan, one of which is in the British Museum.

At the Bauhaus, Wilhelm Wagenfeld, architect and industrial

*...an Puiforcat, who created the ...nusual silver-plated and onyx clock, ...ove, and the handsome silver and ...de soup tureen, right, was France's ...remost silversmith in the Art Deco ...riod. His handsome, classic pieces ...ere fashioned in accordance with his ...otto Le beau dans l'utile (Beauty ... the useful), and his strict adherence ... the Platonic ideal is shown by the ...erfect proportions and geometry of ...s work.*

designer, was associated with the metal workshop from 1922 to about 1931, when he left to work with glass and ceramics. He fashioned a hammered-copper coffee machine in 1923 which is so futuristic in appearance that it could be a prototype for a spaceman's helmet.

Marianne Brandt (b.1893) of the Bauhaus is perhaps the best-known German metalworker. Her designs, although initially guided by geometric principles à la Puiforcat, were far less austere and pristine. One example was a silver teapot she made in 1924, with a hemispherical body, cylindrical lid, semicircular handle and circular ebony knob, all set on four triangular feet. Surprisingly, she turned her supreme design skills to rather mundane objects, such as ashtrays, shaving mirrors and cooking utensils. The most celebrated is her Kandem bedside lamp, which, with its push-button switch and adjustable reflector/shade, is the forerunner of so many lamps today.

In Britain, many established silver firms employed designers who created works in the *moderne* style. Bernard Cuzner (1877–1956) worked in Birmingham and, although grounded in the Arts & Crafts tradition, his pieces – boxes, bowls, etc – in the 1920s and 1930s included those with stylized floral and geometric motifs. The Scot J. Leslie Auld (b.1914), who headed the silver-smithing department at the Glasgow School of Art, designed among other things, commemorative works with Viennese and high-style French overtones, one of which he made for the 1939–40 World's Fair in New York.

The United States was chock-a-block with mass-produced and hand-crafted metalwork, as well as with precious objects made of silver. The latter were based primarily on European design, chiefly derived from the traditional Jensen, but also from the *moderne* Puiforcat. As in France and Britain, established silver firms hired talented designers. The Danish Erik Magnussen (1884–1961), for instance, worked, among others, for the Gorham Manufacturing Company in Rhode Island. His output was sometimes fairly restrained and classic, sometimes exuberantly *moderne*. He produced a covered cup in silver and ivory which is quite Jensen-like; at the other extreme, he created a burnished-silver coffee service with gilt and oxidized angular panels, entitled *The Lights and Shadows of Manhattan*, which is bold, witty and architectural in form.

The German-born Peter Müller-Munk, who moved to New York in 1926, produced wonderful silver designs for many years (his eponymous industrial-design firm still exists). Essentially simple and neo-classical, but with subtle tinges of modernism, his works were supremely crafted. A rectilinear silver tea and coffee service in the Metropolitan Museum of Art has ivory handles that resemble tusks, and is engraved with linear patterns reminiscent of Mayan or Aztec motifs. Other objects, although more rounded and traditional, always contain some unique, modern touch – a wavy gold line, an exaggerated spout, an architectonic pedestal.

*The metal grille, left, is featured in Grays State Theatre, Essex. Like much of the interior metalwork of Art Deco cinemas and skyscrapers, the pattern on the metal grille derive from Parisian creations of the same era.*

*The pewter tobacco box, below, is by Britons A. R. Emerson and A. E. Poulter. Its engraved floral motif and fluted knob are handsome moderne elements.*

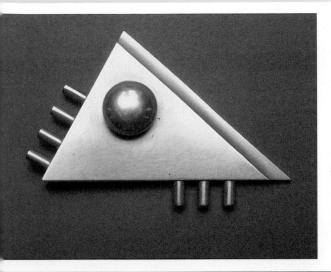

*Georges Fouquet, one of Paris"
foremost jewellers, fashioned the gold
brooch, left. Many of his creations,
with their crisp geometric styling,
displayed a Machine-Age sensibility
far removed from his early Art
Nouveau-period works.*

*Although the sunburst-patterned
compacts, above, look precious, they
are examples of the inexpensive
enamelled- and paste-encrusted-
metal variety. The one on the left is
English, by Stratton, and the
rectangular one by Elizabeth Arden.*

California by the 1920s. His designs for clocks (including digital ones in the 1930s!), lamps, tea and coffee sets and furniture were sleekly moderne but wholly functional. Even the smallest of items, like a stepped clock case of brass and chromed metal, was impeccably designed, undeniably Machine Age. Weber was also a voracious writer on modern design, publishing several thoughtful articles in contemporary journals.

Large-scale metal works in America – gates, architectural elements and such – were much influenced by the Parisian designs of Edgar Brandt, Subes and other *ferronniers*. Brandt himself opened a New York outlet in 1925 and exhibited widely in the United States. The impact of his work can be clearly discerned on the designers at the Rose Iron Works in Cleveland, Ohio, whose screens and tables are blatant imitations.

Many American metalworkers were engaged in gigantic architectural projects for which they often turned to materials other than the traditional iron, bronze, brass and copper. Aluminium, chromium, cadmium and "Monel" metal (a nickel-copper alloy), among others, all came into play, sometimes used as thin sheetings (or plates) over another metal. Numerous components of New York skyscrapers – elevators, mail boxes, doors, etc – were made of these new metals, used either on their own or in combination with other materials. Some of these (often anonymous) creations, with their geometric, floral and figural grillwork, have come to be considered the most outstanding examples of Art Deco in America. Distinguished examples are to be found in New York's Chanin and Daily News buildings, as well as in countless other structures throughout the country. They are discussed further in the architecture section.

**M**any companies – International Silver, Reed & Barton and Tiffany, among others – responded to the call for modernism. Gilbert Rohde and Gene Theobald, two respected industrial designers, created inventive new items for International Silver in Connecticut.

Non-precious metals such as nickel and chrome were also used for tea sets and accessories. The Chase Brass & Copper Company in Waterbury, Connecticut, which employed famous as well as obscure designers, produced a wide range of useful ware known for their "beautility" – cigarette boxes, ashtrays, cocktail shakers, wine coolers, kitchen utensils, candlesticks, vases. Their designs were wonderfully *moderne*, architectonic, Cubist and crisp. A bud vase of 1936, one of which is in New York Metropolitan Museum of Art, consists of four chrome pipes attached to each other at uneven angles and resting on a circular base.

Kem Weber (1889–1963) was born in Berlin, but settled in

The elaborate silvered-bronze and onyx mantel clock, right, was designed around 1930 by Albert Cheuret. The timepiece is one of the handsomest evocations of the Pharaonic era produced during the Egyptian Revival of the 1920s and 30s. Cheuret also designed other clocks, lighting fixtures and bronze figures. Note the stylized numerals on the clock, made up entirely of straight lines.

The wrought-iron mirror, above, was designed by Edgar Brandt in the 1920s. The floral swag is a rococo device, but stylized in the Art Deco mode. The pâte-de-verre lampshades are by Gabriel Argy-Rousseau.

Danish silversmith Georg Jensen influenced many Parisian designers with his ornamental confections, such as the 1921 candelabra, right, embellished with his signature beads of silver.

The Parisian design partnership of Louis Süe and André Mare produced the gilt-bronze clock, below, c.1924. The volute feet and draped face are rococo elements found on other Süe et Mare pieces, including their furniture. Mare was trained as a painter, Süe as an architect.

The box, right, features graceful gazelles leaping amid stylized leafy forms. Deer, gazelles, elands, stags and various other biches (does), as they were collectively called, appeared on a wide variety of Art Déco objects, especially metalwork. This yellow-metal container is actually a powder compact-and-cigarette case, and was made by the Elgin American firm in Illinois.

The lacquer-worker Jean Dunand created the two slender copper vases, above, c.1920–25. They have been gilded and patinated with refined geometric designs.

Jean Puiforcat fashioned the seven-piece silver and ivory tea service, left c.1930. Paris's premier silversmith often embellished his precious-metal work with semiprecious materials, such as ivory, jade and lapis lazuli, as well as with more common materials like wood and glass. The attention Puiforcat paid to the geometric detailing of his pieces can be seen on the subtly fluted sides of the six vessels.

John Paul Cooper, an English architect/silversmith/jeweller, designed the handsome silver and shagreen cigarette box, below, in 1928. Note how the natural dotted pattern of the shark's skin is echoed by the beads of silver which adorn it. Cooper revived the use of sharkskin in fine English metalwork, although its application was much more conservative in Britain.

### JEAN PUIFORCAT

Among the silversmiths working in Art Deco Paris, Jean E. Puiforcat (1897–1945) was the outstanding master. His silver and silver-gilt vessels were smoothly and intelligently crafted objets, often punctuated by handles, finials and knobs of semiprecious stones, ivory, wood and other materials. Some of his later, pure-metal forms could appear futuristic, even architectonic, although the master himself denied being inspired by industry or the machine, adding that the latter was "not French in spirit". He was guided more by philosophical and mathematical formulae, applying them to simple and pristine shapes in his never-ending search for the Platonic ideal of form through mathematical harmony. Indeed, the elaborate and meticulous designs he drew for his pieces were perfectly executed on graph paper – and quite a contrast with the rough sketches produced by so many of his well-known (and equally successful) contemporaries. In 1930 Puiforcat helped found the *Union des Artistes Modernes*, whose collective motto was *Le beau dans l'utile* (Beauty in the useful). This can be seen in all of his pieces, whether a pitcher for the ocean liner *Normandie*, a smart table lamp for Saks Fifth Avenue or a handsome silver and rosewood tea set with tray, today in the collection of the Virginia Museum of Fine Arts, Richmond, US.

Among the unusual materials Jean Dunand employed was coquille d'oeuf, embedded in his vase of 1923–24, left. The use of crushed eggshell by oriental craftsmen on lacquered articles was a technique eagerly adopted by Dunand. The patterns he created with the organic substance could be geometric, as shown, or dazzlingly abstract. Eggshell was used as a substitute for the colour white, which was not naturally available as a resin.

Gilt-silver and onyx make up this finely articulated 1930 bracelet by Jean Despräs, a Parisian jeweller whose works often reflected machine-age, industrial-metal forms. This piece is a precious essay on the circle and the square.

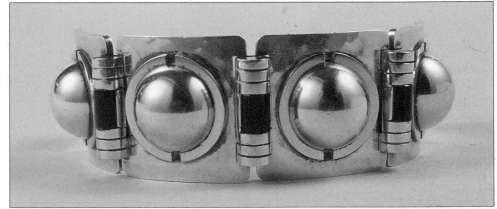

The silvered-bronze, enamel and marble clock, right, was one of 150 or pieces created in enamelled metal Jean Goulden. Goulden, who had studied medicine, visited a Greek monastery while serving in World War I and became enamoured of the Byzantine enamels and icons he saw there. Subsequently he took up the skill of enamelling, which he learned from his friend Jean Dunand. In 1927 Goulden left Paris, settled in Reims and devoted himself to enamelling and decorating clocks, lamps and other objects, usually with distinctive geometric patterns in a Cubist vein.

The silver soup tureen, above, is another masterpiece by Jean Puiforcat. Its carved finial and handles are of lapis lazuli, and its curved body is punctuated by vertical ribs neatly gouged in three places: Puiforcat applied philosophical and mathematical principles to his designs, ever searching for a Platonic ideal of form by means of mathematical harmony.

# FUNCTIONAL

English silversmiths in the Art Deco era wrought stylish, if conservative, pieces; some, however, sported the occasional geometric motif. Below are four round boxes by H. G. Murphy, each topped by a stylish finial; a cigarette box by C. J. Shiner, and a nielloed bowl by Bernard Cuzner, all from the early 30s.

The stirrup-shaped clock, right, was designed by Jaeger Le Coultre for Hermès. The frame is gilded wood, the face red leather, the "numerals" and dials gilt-metal.

German-born Peter Müller-Munk, who emigrated to the United States in 1926, designed the silver-plated pitcher Normandie, left.

The handsome silver-plated metal and ebony tea service, above, was designed by Gilbert Rohde for International Silver in Connecticut;

it was made by the Wilcox Plate Co. The talents of an industrial designer such as Rohde are shown by its well-engineered, compact design.

The designer of the lovely enamelled metal powder compact, below, is unknown; it was made for the American cosmetics firm Richard Hudnut. Its incised design, of a stylized Egyptian lotus, is simple yet stylish – but for its mundane materials, it could have been designed by a skilful silversmith.

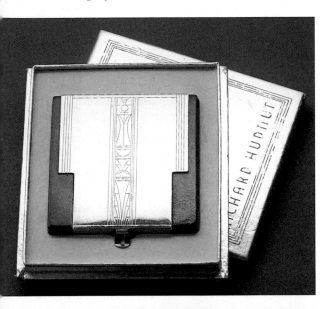

Commemorative silverware was a popular souvenir in the 1920s and 30s. Left, four spoons from a set of 12 celebrating the 1939 New York World's Fair. The architectural theme of the Fair, the Trylon and Perisphere, appears at the top of each handle, and the different exhibition buildings on the bowls. The spoons are silver-plated, and were made by the Wm Rogers Mfg Co, which was connected with International Silver of Meriden, Connecticut.

Raymond Templier designed the lacquered-silver cigarette case, right, in 1930. Its elaborate geometric pattern resembles those found on bookbindings and carpets. The red and black palette was a common one used in Art Deco Paris.

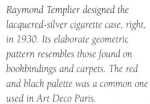

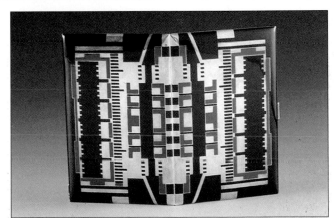

Far from the geographical centre of Art Deco, an Indian silversmith fashioned the lovely tea set, right, after an English design. Note especially the attached bases, eliminating the need for a trivet.

Although its shape is prophetic of a rocket ship, the silver-plated cocktail maker, above, with its six goblets, was, in 1920s Paris, merely moderne.

It was designed by Desny, and was also available in solid silver, with a matching tray.

# FORGED METAL

*This practical and decorative metallic grille at the Phoenix Cinema in East Finchley, London was probably not hand-forged. But even so, it resembles a segment of precious Parisian wrought-iron work, and it even seems to possess three dimensions, not just two.*

## EDGAR BRANDT

The best-known ironworker in Art Deco Paris was the Alsatian-born Edgar Brandt (1880–1960), who began working in metal at 15 and who set up his own studio in 1919 after studying with the noted ironworker Emile Robert. Often collaborating with architects and *ensembliers*, Brandt produced a large quantity and huge variety of ornamental metalwork, ranging from utilitarian objects such as urns, firedogs, lamps, mirrors and tables, to interior and exterior architectural metalwork, including gates, screens, grilles and such. His works were made of iron, copper, brass, bronze, and even aluminium, sometimes patinated. He also produced silver and gold jewellery early in his career, making him a true "man of all metals".

He designed a multitude of objects for the 1925 Paris Exposition, among them architectural elements for his own pavilion and for those of other designers and firms. He received public and private commissions from France and abroad, and he set up a New York branch of his firm, which he called Ferrobrandt and which was run by ironworker Jules Bouy. Among his North American commissions were the main entrance, window frames and other design elements for New York's Madison-Belmont Building, on Madison Avenue and 34th Street; a complete showroom for the fabric makers Cheney Brothers, in the same building; and the entrance door to the Montreal Chamber of Commerce. He also designed lift panels for Selfridges, Oxford Street, London, in 1928 (the panels are today in the collection of the Brighton Art Gallery and Museums).

*The wrought-iron gates, left, by Edgar Brandt, date from c.1929. They were once located at the entrance to a building on Paris's Rue Geynemer designed by Michel Roux-Spitz. The cast-iron medallions centring each of the gates depict faces which may represent night and day or summer and winter. Brandt's triumph at the 1925 Paris Exposition, for which he designed much of the ornamental ironwork, led to numerous commissions both in France and abroad.*

Classical volutes figure on this hammered wrought-iron urn by Edgar Brandt, which measures some 20in (50cm) across. Although on first glance deceptively simple-looking, the urn shows impeccable craftsmanship; the soft, ribbony quality of the bent metal could be achieved only by the most skilful of metalsmiths.

The bronze grille, below, is from the Circle Tower Building, Indianapolis, completed in 1938. With its prancing gazelles and geometric devices, the grille is in the style of Edgar Brandt, who by 1925 had opened Ferrobrandt, the New York branch of his Paris firm.

The green-patinated-bronze standard lamp, above, is by Armand-Albert Rateau. The birds are classical devices adopted by Rateau. Several of the lamps were in the Paris home of couturière Jeanne Lanvin, most of which was furnished by Rateau between 1920 and 1922.

The wrought-iron table, above, with a top of grey granite, is attributed to Raymond Subes who, like Edgar Brandt, served an apprenticeship with the ironworker Emile Robert. Like Brandt, he also produced a variety of ornamental gates, screens, grilles, etc, for the 1925 Paris Exposition. The table pictured has a much sparer decoration than most other Parisian metalwork of the period. Note the nude figure with fruit bowl highlighted in red ochre on the table top.

# COLOUR

The copper vase, below, is by Claudius Linossier. Its hammered and patinated surface is embellished with a pattern of silver spirals. Such types of vessel are termed dinanderie (from the Belgian town, Dinant), and their production involves shaping sheets of copper, pewter or other metals with a mallet, then decoratin them in any number of ways – chasing, embossing, inlay, etc.

The jewel-like enamel-on-copper vase, above, is by Camille Fauré, the great Art Deco enamellist. The stylized floral pattern is atypical for Fauré, whose vessels usually were covered with strong geometric designs, as on the next page. The enamelling process entails combining pulverized glass with chemical pigments, the resultant powder then being mixed with an adhesive and fused to a metal base in a c.1,500°F (800°C) kiln.

The monochromatic inner and outer surfaces of the vividly hued lacquered metal bowl, right, are rather unusual for Jean Dunand, whose pieces generally were decorated with geometric patterns.

Camille Fauré created the trio of colourful enamelled vases, left. Their designs are typical Art Deco motifs: left, stylized leaves; in the centre, geometric shapes; and right, an array of semicircles. The middle vase is also highlighted with silver.

The lacquered metal vase, below, with its sophisticated, asymmetrical stripe design in red and black, is by Jean Dunand. It stands on a Macassar ebony pedestal by Clément Rousseau, whose furniture was delicate yet solid, and always luxurious.

A lively but spare geometric pattern has been enamelled onto the box, left, by Jean Goulden. The zigzag, or lightning-bolt, pattern is a common Art Deco device, as is the dentate row of squares, which here are painted in green and blue. Goulden gave up medicine to pursue a career in enamelling, a technique he learned from his friend and sometime collaborator Jean Dunand.

*Faience vase by René Buthaud, France, 1925*

# CHAPTER • THREE
# CERAMICS

Geometry was a keyword in Art Deco ceramics, from the ovals and orbs dominating the shapes of French glazed stoneware to the triangles and circles decorating pots in England, the United States, Germany and even Russia. But added to a rigid geometric form, there could be a stylized floral design, a frieze of deer, or great whorls of bright colour. Sometimes those geometric patterns were to be found on irregularly shaped vessels – zigzagged vases and sugar bowls or cups with triangular (and hard to grasp) ears. Art Deco ceramics could also take the form of ebullient, sensuous or humorous figures: dancing couples in vivid costumes, earthenware female busts with corkscrew curls, smiling pigs with purple spots.

The most serene and classical ceramics of the period emanated from France, where the names René Buthaud, Jean Mayodon, Jean Besnard, and especially Emile Decoeur and Emile Lenoble reigned supreme. Decoeur (1876–1953) was a potter who worked in faïence, stoneware and porcelain. Before 1920 his vessels were generally decorated with geometric or floral designs which later gave way to heavy, pale-coloured glazes. These were sometimes mottled, sometimes tinged with darker hues at the rim, but always applied to traditionally shaped vessels.

Lenoble (1876–1940), on the other hand, almost always decorated his classical forms with floral and abstract designs, as well as with coloured *craquelure* glazes, similar to those found on Sung Chinese and Korean pottery. His stylized motifs could be moulded in a subtle bas-relief; incised in the applied slip or clay, or painted over or under the glaze. The glazes on his stoneware were often earthy in tone – greens, reds, browns, whites – but the stylized decorations, whether subtle or strong, distinguished the pieces from the works of his contemporaries.

René Buthaud, Jean Mayodon and Jean Besnard were painters or decorators of earthenware. Besnard's decorations were generally subdued and geometric, but often highlighted with silver or gold. Mayodon hand-shaped or painted his designs on vessels; human figures, birds or deer frequent his work, and he sometimes applied gold lustre, as in Middle Eastern ceramics. René Buthaud's designs are perhaps the strongest of the three, and his boldly outlined, female forms are especially distinctive.

Mass-produced tableware in both porcelain and earthenware, with handsome Art Deco motifs, also emerged from France. Among the designers were Suzanne Lalique, René's daughter, who worked for Théodore Haviland at Limoges (she also married into the Haviland family); Marcel Goupy, who also designed for Limoges; and Jean Luce, who displayed lovely white porcelain plates with a silver and gold cloud and sunray motif at the 1925 Paris Exposition. Established factories such as Sèvres produced Art Deco porcelain, including elegant vases with stylized floral designs and monumental display pieces – a huge ginger jar, for instance, created for the 1937 *Exposition Internationale des arts et Techniques* in Paris and covered with a lush tropical scene in pastel shades of pink, blue, green and beige.

Such well-known *ensembliers* as Emile-Jacques Ruhlmann (see

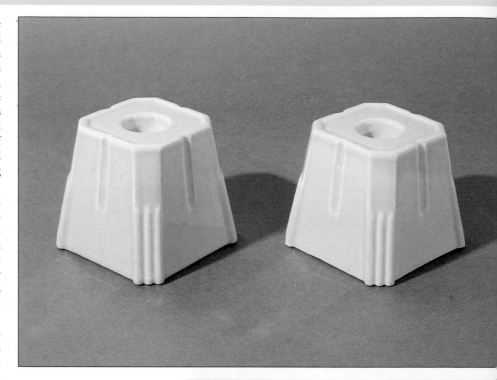

*The ceramic candleholders above were made by the National Porcelain Co of Trenton, New Jersey. Their stepped, pyramidal shape echoes that of other Mayan-influenced objects of the Art Deco period.*

*One of Paris's premier ceramicists was Emile Lenoble. His shapes were often derived from classic oriental vessels, as were many of his glazes, such as the craquelure-yellow surface on the stoneware vase, right.*

the chapter on furniture) were connected with porcelain as well a delicate cream-coloured cup and saucer with touches of gold were made to his design by Sèvres. The faïence factory Longw also produced Art Deco designs and sold them through the Atelie Primavera of the Parisian store Au Printemps. Primavera's cerami section was directed from 1923 to 1926 by René Buthaud, ano among its output were outstanding earthenware sculptures o animals splashed with mottled enamels in various colours; monumental green- and black-enamelled bison and a frisk stylized horse in white and cream were part of the menageri which Primavera offered up for sale.

# CERAMICS

In England, two names are synonymous with Art Deco ceramics, Clarice Cliff and Susie Cooper. Their creations were quite antithetical to those of the French designers, but their assured use of colours and designs, as well as their sheer exuberance – and their commercial success – give them a rightful place in Art Deco design.

Clarice Cliff (1899–1972) studied at the Burslem School of Art and began her career as a decorator at A.J. Wilkinson's Royal Staffordshire pottery. In 1928 her *so-called Bizarre* ware was triumphantly introduced to the public. The cups and saucers, bowls, platters, vases and other pieces bore strong, simple designs – flowers, landscapes, geometric patterns – in bright hues, including vivid colours hitherto undreamed of in British ceramics, such as purple and a shade of orange she called "tango". Their shapes were usually traditional, but some of them sported angular stems or feet. She also decorated limited-edition pieces; among her most distinctively Art Deco was a series of plaques known as the *Age of Jazz,* ceramic cut-outs which featured black-tie-clad musicians and colourful dancing couples. She was known to admire the designs and colours of the Ballets Russes, and a rare plaque pays homage to Diaghilev's dance company. During her career, she hired well-known artists and sculptors, including Graham Sutherland, Paul Nash, Laura Knight, Barbara Hepworth and Ben Nicholson, to design tableware for the Wilkinson and Newport companies.

Susie Cooper (b.1902), like Clarice Cliff, studied at the Burslem School. In 1922 she began work at A. E. Gray & Co, soon becoming their resident designer. When she was 29 she set up her own company and in 1931 the firm Wood & Son decided to supply her with shapes to decorate, a move that proved positive for both parties. Department stores such as Selfridges and John Lewis sold her wares, whose colours and patterns were generally of subdued, muted tones – greens, blues, pinks and beiges. Her tableware bore designs of stylized leaves, wispy ribbons, concentric circles and sometimes elegant animals. Some large pieces were brightly coloured and had bolder animal or floral motifs, but the vast majority of her output was lighter, simpler – and ultimately classier than Clarice Cliff's work.

*Britain's best-known ceramics designer, Clarice Cliff, created both the vivid fruit-patterned plate above, and the chic dancing couple on the left (part of her Age of Jazz series of cut-out figures). Cliff's colours and patterns were bold, lively and extremely popular in her own day – as they are with collectors today.*

In the wake of the success of these two innovative ceramicists, many English potteries – both established and new – began to produce tableware in the modern vein. Doulton, Shelley, Carlton, Crown Devon, Pilkingtons and Wedgwood all climbed on the bandwagon, the last employing Keith Murray, who also worked in glass, to design some lovely, subtle vessels for them. Carter, Stabler & Adams, which was formed in Poole in 1921, created painted earthenware boasting exuberant floral and geometric designs in colours that were vivid but quite distinctive from those of Clarice Cliff.

Also working in Britain in the 1920s and 1930s was a new breed of studio potter – Bernard Leach, William Staite-Murray, Shoji Hamada, Michael Cardew, Lucie Rie, Hans Coper, Katharine Pleydell Bouverie. They all eschewed mass-production methods,

# CERAMICS

bright colours and modern motifs in favour of earthy glazes, slip decoration and other traditional but timeless techniques, designs and forms essentially grounded in classic oriental ceramics.

Slightly less traditional and more eccentric had been the painted pottery and tin-glazed earthenware of the Omega Workshops (1913–19), set up in London by Roger Fry, who himself made their earthenware at Camberwell and Poole. Vanessa Bell and Duncan Grant painted decorations on their vases and platters as well; they were pretty and brightly coloured, but overall rather elementary, with a childish charm. Still, these two artists were later invited by Clarice Cliff to join the talented coterie who designed tableware for her.

Art Deco-style pottery and porcelain were produced in virtually every other western country, as well as in Japan and in post-Revolutionary Russia, where it was under the aegis of the reorganized State Porcelain Manufactory. The plates, cup and saucers and other utilitarian ware designed by Nikolai Suetin, Vladimir Tatlin and Kasimir Malevich, among others, were perhaps the ultimate in Art Deco design. The Russians claimed to take Cubism one step further, making it an absolutely pure geometrical abstract art. The patterns adorning the almost invariably white grounds were indeed bold, geometric statements: circles, rectangles, straight lines and other pure shapes in strong shades – red, black, grey. However, they were asymmetrically placed in a deliberate unbalance, making them quite distinct from French designs. The Russian pavilion at the 1925 Paris Exposition, which featured these "propagandist pots", proved quite a success with Westerners, as did the paintings, collages and graphics created by these same artists. The Art Deco designs exported to the West from Japan, on the other hand, on vases and assorted tableware, were often traditional Japanese motifs – elegant birds and landscapes – translated into modern terms and duly stylized.

A healthy ceramic industry also existed elsewhere in Eastern Europe, where firms such as Rosenthal in Bavaria and Royal Dux (Duxer Porzellanmanufaktur) in Bohemia produced vases, figurines and other porcelain *objets*, often in blatant imitation of the Gallic style. At the opposite end of the scale, the Bauhaus ceramic section in Germany was headed by Gerhard Marcks. at first, unglazed low-fired earthenware was made, in simple shapes and often with exaggerated spouts and lips, boldly emphasizing the beauty of the medium; later dark glazes were employed, especially by Theodor Bogler, and Richard Bampi, who was inspired by Chinese ceramics.

In Austria the Vereinigte Wiener und Gmundner Keramik company, established by Berthold Löffler and Michael Powolny in 1905 (as the Wiener Keramik), created vases, sculptures and various vessels with the stylized-floral and geometric designs characteristic of the Wiener Werkstätte. Susi Singer and Vally Wieselthier, two ceramicists of note, who joined the Wiene Werkstätte's Kunstlerwerkstätte in 1920, produced rough-textured colourful figures and vases of glazed clay, many of

*The jar and cover, above, are by the Royal Doulton pottery of Burslem, Staffordshire. The oriental floral and bird motif, the vessel's shape, and the glaze covering it – a flambé -type Doulton termed Sung glaze – are all derived from Chinese ceramics.*

women with strong features, almond eyes and high-arched brows These were innovative and exciting, sometimes comic, sometime sultry, but ever fascinating.

The Danish Bing & Grøndahl and Royal Copenhagen porcelai factories also contributed designs in the Art Deco style, as di Boch Frères in Belgium Società Ceramica Richard-Ginori was th leading maker, employing the gifted architect and furnitur designer Gio Ponti from 1923.

American pottery, although not as innovative and exciting a the "art pottery" produced in the Art Nouveau and Arts & Craft

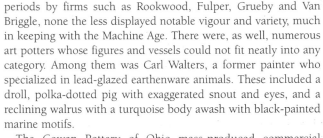

*New Zealand-born Keith Murray designed pieces for several UK potteries, including the two lovely vases, left, for Wedgwood.*

*The glazed-ceramic figures, below, are by American Waylande de Santis Gregory. In the centre is Salome, and on the right is Radio, bearing a lightning-bolt (a common symbol of communication in the 1920s and 30s).*

periods by firms such as Rookwood, Fulper, Grueby and Van Briggle, none the less displayed notable vigour and variety, much in keeping with the Machine Age. There were, as well, numerous art potters whose figures and vessels could not fit neatly into any category. Among them was Carl Walters, a former painter who specialized in lead-glazed earthenware animals. These included a droll, polka-dotted pig with exaggerated snout and eyes, and a reclining walrus with a turquoise body awash with black-painted marine motifs.

The Cowan Pottery of Ohio mass-produced commercial ceramic figures which in effect elevated the craft into a fine art, at least in the eyes of some critics. Although many of Cowan's designers were influenced by Viennese pottery, their figures were far more abstract and sleeker. Two stand out: pelican-head book ends by A. Drexel Jacobson and *Bird and Wave* by Alexandre Blazys, which depicts, improbably, a peacock astride the sea. Another Cowan employee, Viktor Schreckengost, who had studied in Vienna, produced black and turquoise porcelain bowls with carved motifs which are outstanding evocations of the Jazz Age – mélanges of skyscrapers, sunbursts, circles and stars and neon signs. William Hunt Diederich (1884–1953), who also worked in metal, developed an interest in ceramics while travelling in Morocco in the 1920s. After collecting and studying indigenous North African pottery, he began to paint and glaze his own earthenware. Among his most distinguished expressions were a wrought-iron chandelier and a ceramic plate, both inspired by the same ancient Mesopotamian motif and featuring a pair of rearing ibexes. As in other countries, the Unite States had its fair share of designers and factories which are forgotten or anonymous today, but admired and collected none the less for their attractive designs. Colourful female faces and figures, angular vases and bowls, tableware with handsome geometric patterns, sometimes even hand-painted – the output of these firms was vast and diverse, providing a significant contribution to Art Deco ceramics.

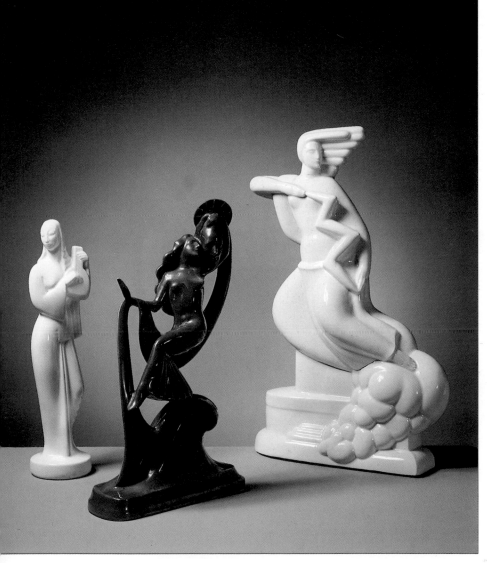

# MOTIFS

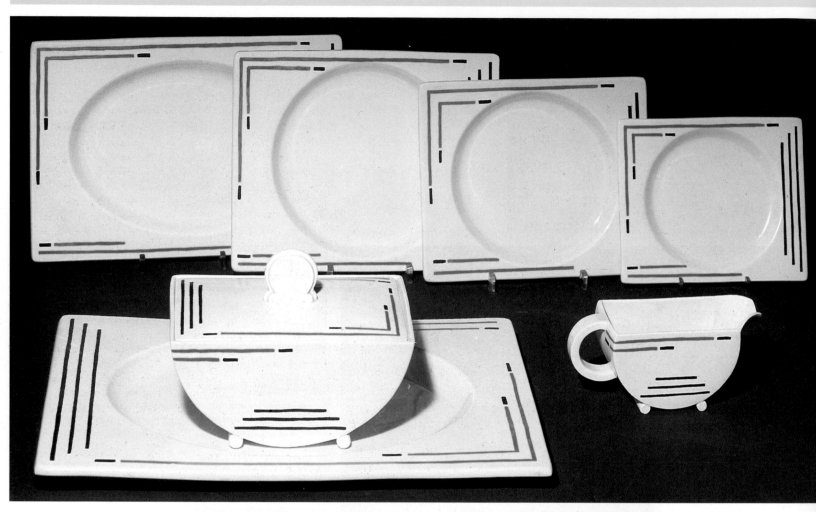

The English tea service, above, dates from 1934 and was designed by Clarice Cliff. One of the Biarritz line, the minimally decorated set is perhaps her most geometric. She was better known for her brightly hued, exuberantly painted ceramics, in part influenced by the colours and designs of the Ballets Russes. The spare, hand-painted black and red lines perfectly complement the pure rectangular and round shapes.

Left is a partial table setting by Susie Cooper in the Dresden Spray pattern of c.1935, which was a contemporary interpretation of a traditional Staffordshire floral design. The central motif was transfer-printed on each piece, and the shaded bands were available in various pastel hues. Susie Cooper's long career has spanned over 60 years, and she has remained an important figure in British ceramics through the decades.

The three pieces of anonymous French porcelain, left, are glided along the edge and painted with a circle-and-ray design. Their shapes, unlike their decorations, are traditional.

## SUSIE COOPER

Susie Cooper (b. 1902), unlike her fellow British ceramics designer Clarice Cliff, not only created lovely, distinctive designs on a wide variety of tableware, but she also had her own company. From 1929 she ran the Susie Cooper Pottery, having been employed by the decorating firm E. E. Gray & Co prior to that; in 1966, her firm became part of the Wedgwood Group. At Gray's Pottery, Susie Cooper – who had studied drawing and sculpture, but never ceramics design, in her native Burslem, Staffordshire – contributed floral, figural, geometric and ringed designs, hand-painting them on jars, jugs, statuettes and tableware. Some of her loveliest hand-painted pieces were decorated with various biches – ibex, deer, rams – very much in the prevalent Parisian style. She also painted lustred designs on earthenware, sometimes with traditional Islamic devices. But by far her most successful designs were simply banded, dotted or otherwise sparely embellished, usually in muted hues – pastels or earthy tones – on cream grounds, that is, bone china. Likewise, the techniques she used on her mass-produced tableware – over-glaze and under-glaze, transfer-printing and aerography, and many more, either singly combination – earned her the respect of many of her contemporaries. She received the OBE in 1979, four decades after being designated a Royal Designer for Industry in 1940, the only woman ever to be so recognized for her contribution to pottery design.

though its strong geometric design oks very 1920s, the coffee service ove dates from 1911. The set is an ample of Czech Cubism, a ovement which permeated design in at Eastern European country in the 910s. It is signed "Artěl".

The jaunty teapot, right, is by the Hall China Company, an American firm which mass-produced tableware. Covered in Chinese red glaze, the swag-like form is called Rhythm (1939).

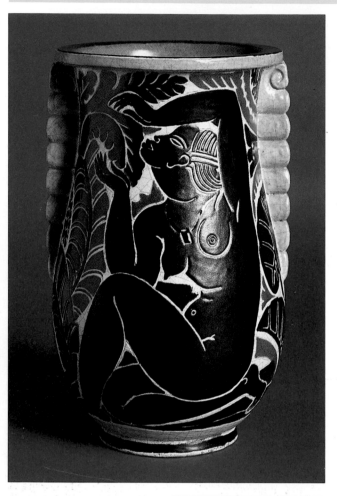

One of the premier ceramics designers in Art Deco France was René Buthaud, who created the stoneware vase, left, with its exotic Negro figure. Buthaud executed this piece after attending the 1931 Exposition Coloniale in Paris, where much African art had been on display.

The porcelain plate, right, was designed by Jean Luce for display at the 1925 Paris Exposition. Its simple floral/geometric motif is highlighted in gold. A technical adviser for the Sèvres factory, Luce also designed glass and porcelain for the ocean liner Normandie.

Jean Mayodon designed and painted the faïence bowl with polychrome glazes, right, covering it all over with massive figures and beasts derived from Greek mythology, one of his favourite subjects. Mayodon, who was influenced as well by Middle Eastern pottery techniques, had first studied painting.

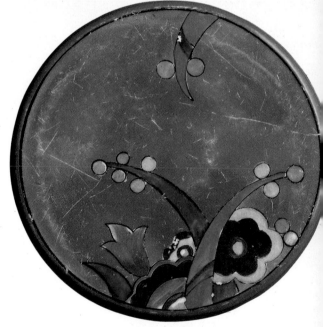

The hand-painted plaque, above, is by Noritake, a Japanese ceramics factory established in Nagoya in 1904. Much of the firm's export ware in the 1930s was decorated with distinctly moderne patterns, as the stylized floral design on this piece illustrates.

The ceramic trinket box, left, is probably English. Both its central floral medallion and leafy gold borders have been transfer-printed onto a blank body, in the manner of so much mass-produced pottery in the 1920s and 30s.

Parisian ceramicist Emile Lenoble designed the turned stoneware vase, right; its floral design was overlaid in slip.

The American Henry Varnum Poor designed and executed the glazed-earthenware plate, left, c.1930. In 1910–11, Poor studied in London and Paris, afterwards returning to teach painting at California's Stanford University.

The Sèvres factory created the ceramic barrel, right, c.1920. The monkey finial resembles a Japanese netsuke, enhancing its overall oriental look.

Diana Cacciatrice, *or* Diana the Hunter, *the ceramic figure on the left, was modelled by Angelo Biancini for the Societa Ceramica Italiania in Laveno-Mombello, a porcelain centre on Lake Maggiore. Dating from 1935–38, the sculpture is nearly 3ft (91 cm) high.*

*The white-glazed earthenware figure, right, was made in the 1920s by Ashtead Pottery, Surrey, which employed disabled World War I veterans. The overall appearance of the girl and the floral-swagged plinth are similar to Viennese pottery of the same time.*

*Atelier Primavera, the design studio attached to the Paris store Au Printemps, produced the earthenware horse, below. Its highly textured glazing is typical of many Primavera sculptures.*

The highly decorative glazed-earthenware figures, below, by Serapis-Fayence, Vienna, are very much in the style of Wiener Keramik artist Michael Powolny. Serapis was founded in 1863 by Bohemian potter Ernst Wahliss; from 1911 his sons, Hans and Erich, began to produce figures such as those shown.

The earthenware bison, below, is by Primavera and is glazed in black and mottled green, the latter resembling the natural patination on bronze.

British ceramics designer Clarice Cliff created the charming musical duo, above, part of her Age of Jazz series of cut-out, painted figures, which also included colourful dancing couples.

# COLOUR

The Belgian pottery Boch Frères, a branch of the German firm Villeroy & Boch, established the Keramis factory at La Louvière in 1841. In the 1920s Keramis produced vessels decorated in the Art Deco style, such as the group at right, some of them by Parisian designer Marcel Goupy. The craquelure grounds which can be seen on the trio of patterned pieces were deliberate technical devices, adapted from oriental ceramics. The vivid eggyolk-yellow glaze of the same three pieces is quite modern, however.

The British pottery Carter, Stabler & Adams made the colourful earthenware vase, left. The Poole firm's hand-thrown, hand-decorated pots were usually painted by co-founder Harold Stabler or his wife, Phoebe, in distinctive floral or geometric patterns on cream backgrounds.

The porcelain flock, right, was designed by sculptor Edouard-Marcel Sandoz and executed at Limoges by Haviland. Better known as an animalier sculptor in bronze, Sandoz did design a whole series of colourful zoomorphic vessels for Haviland in the late 1920s.

*The 2ft (61cm) high ginger jar, left, was produced by Sèvres and painted by Anne-Marie Fontaine, probably for display at the 1937 Exposition Internationale des Arts et Techniques in Paris. The pot bears a lush tropical scene in creamy pastel glazes.*

## CLARICE CLIFF

The best-known name in Art Deco ceramics, probably even more recognizable than any of the Parisian potters, is that of Clarice Cliff (1900–1972), a Staffordshire-born designer whose brightly hued tableware has come to be considered by many as the greatest manifestation of the Art Deco style in the United Kingdom. She trained at the Burslem School of Art, and then served an apprenticeship with A. J. Wilkinson, who appointed her director of their Royal Staffordshire Pottery and Newport Pottery subsidiary in 1939. Besides painting her own designs on often partly or wholly angular-shaped forms, she also took the designs of well-known British artists – Frank Brangwyn, Paul Nash, Laura Knight, Graham Sutherland and Duncan Grant, among them – and translated them on to plates, cups, vases and other items. Her own distinctive glazes and designs are what she is best known for, and these were often bright, bold patterns influenced by the stage sets and costumes of Sergei Diaghilev's Ballets Russes, which made such an impact in Western Europe in the Art Deco era. Her *Bizarre, Crocus, Biarritz* and *Fantasque* lines endeared the public to her, and it is safe to assume that her tableware literally brightened the dreary days of many a Briton. Stylized floral motifs, stark banded designs, fantasy landscapes, geometric configurations and even some rather abstract, painterly devices adorned her most popular pottery. There were also special, limited-edition pieces, such as her *Age of Jazz* series, which comprised cut-out painted figures of tangoing couples and tuxedoed musicians. Her palette included greens, blues, scarlets, oranges and purples, and sometimes all these hues would converge on a vase featuring zigzags and solid rings. Clarice Cliff's pottery was exported to Australia, New Zealand and other countries, and several of her designs are being reproduced today.

*The pottery group, right, is by Clarice Cliff. The deep orange hue, which designers of the day called Tango, predominates, as do bold motifs – geometric, floral and banded. Clarice Cliff's palette was largely influenced by the vivid colours of the Ballets Russes.*

Studio-potter Michael Cardew, who had studied with Bernard Leach in St Ives, decorated the 1930s slipware dish, which was moulded by Elijah Comfort at Cardew's Winchcombe Pottery in the Cotswolds. Much of Cardew's work was influenced by Africa, where he taught for over 20 years.

The vase, left, 20in (50.5cm) in diameter, is by the German-born potter Hans Coper, who since 1946 has collaborated in England with Viennese-trained Lucie Rie, another refugee. Their stoneware pieces are extremely functional and modern, usually in neutral tones of white, cream, brown or black.

The Flambé earthenware vase, right, was made by Royal Doulton at Burslem, c.1925. Although its stylized-floral motif is not in the Parisian Art Deco vein, the Far Eastern-inspired red-flambé glaze is in keeping with French ceramics, which were richly decorated in the Oriental manner.

The vases, far right, are from the Futura line of the Roseville Pottery Co, Ohio, introduced in 1924 and produced through the 1930s. Although not as well known or innovative as some of the other Midwestern art potters, Roseville's ware is highly collectable. The glazes on these vases are earthy in tonality, but other Futura vessels came in bright pink and blue.

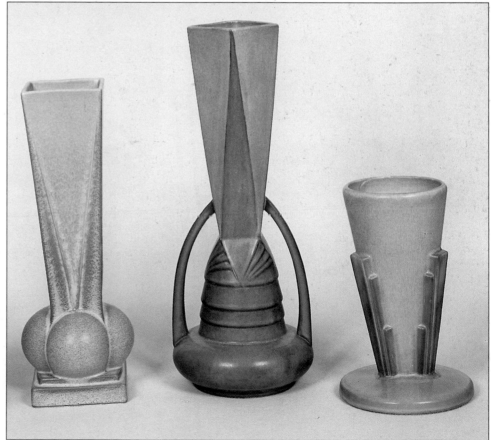

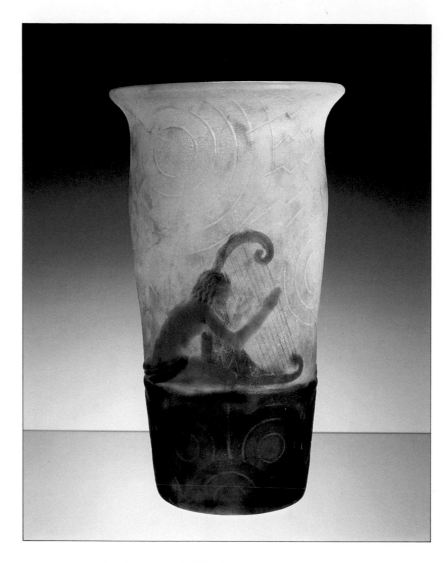

*Pâte-de-verre vase by Gabriel Argy-Rousseau, France, c.1925*

# CHAPTER • FOUR
# GLASS

Glass produced during the Art Deco period ranged from the serene, hand-blown vessels of Maurice Marinot in France and the delicately engraved Graal glass of the Swedes, Hald and Gate, to the perfume bottles of Baccarat and the tableware of America's Libbey Glass Company. In addition, massive panels of stained glass and *verre-églomisé* (glass painted on the reverse side) were produced for homes, churches and ocean liners.

In France, the two major names and influences were Maurice Marinot (1882–1960) and René Lalique (1860–1945). Marinot started and ended his working life as a painter, becoming a member of the renegade Fauve group, known for their wild and colourful canvases. But between 1911 and 1937, he devoted himself to the art of glassmaking. His most exemplary vases, jars and bottles – he produced some 2,500 in all – were thick-walled, stunning objects which elevated the medium of glass to new artistic heights. By emphasizing its actual physical qualities, by seeming miraculously to trap its fluidity in three dimensions, he produced pieces that captivated critics and public alike. What had hitherto been considered flaws in the medium – bubbles, specks of chemicals needed to produce colour and so on – he turned into primary decorative components. These elements, coupled with the traditional ovoid, spherical and squarish forms that so many Art Deco vessels assumed (metal and ceramic, as well as glass), resulted in some of the most beautiful *objets d'art* of the period. He also submerged pieces in acid baths to create deeply etched designs, and produced multi-layered works with various colours or streaks contained within the separate layers.

Marinot had his imitators and followers, not only in his native country (these included Henri Navarre, Georges Dumoulin and André Thuret) but also in other parts of the world. He strongly influenced, for instance, Monart ware, made by Moncrieff's Glass Works in Perth, Scotland, and some of Steuben's lines in the United States, notably Cluthra and Cintra. But his own vessels far surpassed those of his competitors and disciples. Indeed it was he who set the stage for the great studio glassmakers who were to shine some four decades later in the United States, Dominic Labino and Harvey Littleton among them.

Many of Marinot's early pieces – produced from about 1912 to 1922 – were decorated with colourful enamelled designs, usually flowers, sometimes figures. Other Frenchmen, such as Auguste Heiligenstein, Jean Luce and Marcel Goupy (he also worked in ceramics), carried this type of design even further. Much of Goupy's first glassware was covered with stylized flowers, although he later turned to plainer, more geometric motifs.

René Lalique, who was the undisputed *maître verrier* of the Art Deco period, had had a successful earlier career as the premier Art Nouveau goldsmith. Besides designing perfume bottles for Coty, D'Orsay, Worth and at least two dozen other *parfumeurs*, he produced countless boxes, figures (including automobile mascots), vases, clock and picture frames and tableware mostly in his own characteristic heavy glass, which had

# GLASS

René Lalique's 1929 panels for a
Pullman Car on the French Côte
d'Azur train, right, depict elegant
neo-classical nudes amid grapes.
The master glassmaker received many
architectural commissions from
France and abroad during his long
career.

a luminous opalescent appearance. He also created one-of-a-kind vessels in *cire-perdue* (lost wax) glass, as well as monumental architectural pieces, including figural panels for Claridge's hotel in London and John Wanamaker's department store in Philadelphia.

Lalique's forms, techniques, designs and runaway success encouraged many to imitate him, including Sabino Verlys, d'Avesn, Hunebelle and Etling in France, Jobling in England, Val Saint-Lambert in Belgium, Leerdam in Holland, Barolac in Czechoslovakia and the Phoenix and Consolidated Lamp and Glass companies in the United States. But his peerless production methods could never be duplicated, and he guarded his technical secrets closely. His repertory of subjects ranged from sentimental neo-classical nudes to bold, geometric patterns, and some of his finest Art Deco creations are his monumental coloured vases – for example, *Tortues*, with its pattern of billowing tortoises' backs approaching a stark abstraction, and *Tourbillons*, or *Whirlwinds*, a black-enamelled version of which was displayed at the 1925 Paris Exposition. His figures *Suzanne* and *Thaïs* are sensuous, scantily clad symbols of gaiety and abandon, while his mascot *Victoire*, or as it is known in English *Spirit of the Wind*, with her androgynous face and windswept geometricized hairstyle has become something of an icon of Art Deco.

Other French glassmakers enthusiastically embraced Art Deco, including the esteemed Daum Frères which had produced Art Nouveau glass in the 1880s and 1890s in the naturalistic style of Emile Gallé. In the 1930s, the factory created etched-glass wares very much in the contemporary vein, with geometric and stylized-floral patterns often reminiscent of Marinot's vessels, but usually more colourful and decorative. Charles Schneider, who occasionally designed for Daum, founded his own Cristallerie Schneider in 1913, and he became known for his *intercalaires*; coloured inclusions sandwiched between two layers of glass. His works were signed *Charder* (derived from his first and last names), *Le Verre Français* or, simply, *Schneider*.

The group of vases, above, shows the
range of colour, shapes and motifs
found on the vessels of French
glassmaker René Lalique. From left to
right are Archers, Ceylan, Sauge
(Sage) and Ronces (Brambles).

The vase, left, c.1921, is by
Frenchman Charles Schneider. The
applied handles are unusual, but the
flecks of colour in the body are
reminiscent of Marinot's work.
Schneider is known for his
intercalaires, (which contain shots
of colour between their two layers).

The ancient Egyptian technique of *pâte-de-verre* – powdered glass made into a paste with water and a fluxing medium, and then refired in a mould – had been revived at the turn of the century by Henri Cros, and several Art Deco glassmakers continued to employ the process. Foremost among them was François-Emile Décorchement (1880–1971), who also produced near-transparent *pâte-de-cristal* vessels by using a higher percentage of lead. Many of his massive, thick-walled pieces were decorated with stylized floral or faunal motifs and some had animal or figural handles. He also made great use of colour and produced heavy vessels resembling marble or semi-precious stones, an effect he achieved by chemical streaking within the glass. He even stimulated tortoiseshell with a lovely golden-brown glass. His grandsons, Antoine and Etienne Leperlier, have followed in his footsteps and are at work in France today as *pâte-de-verre* artists. They have combined the craft they learned from their grandfather with their own modern design sensibilities to create startlingly contemporary, sculptural glass.

*The above vase, with its stylized floral pattern, was created by Gabriel Argy-Rousseau. Its mottled effect was achieved in the pâte-de-verre process, where glass is ground into a paste with other ingredients and fired in a mould.*

Gabriel Argy-Rousseau (1885–1953) also produced *pâte-de-verre* and *pâte-de-cristal* glass, including small lamps and three-dimensional neo-classical figures, usually of dancers, some modelled by sculptor Marcel Bouraine. Argy-Rousseau's vessels were less massive and more delicate than Décorchement's; indeed floral and figural decorations on pieces dating from the 1910s were sometimes more reminiscent of Art Nouveau. However, the motifs he produced after the First World War – stylized female heads, classical masks, elegant gazelles or floral forms – were more in keeping with 1920s French style. Alméric Walter (1859–1942) was another *pâte-de-verre* designer whose career spanned the Art Nouveau and Art Deco periods. He collaborated with the sculptors Henri Bergé and Jean Descomps, and at one point he worked for Daum. The most Art Deco of his creations are stunning figures, veiled women dancers in dramatic poses.

Some superb stained glass works were produced in France in the Art Deco style, including windows and panels by Maurice Jallot, J. Gaudin, Gaétan Jeannin and Jacques Grube (1870–1936), the last of whom had produced stunning Art Nouveau designs as well. A series of windows with sports players – one features a jaunty lady golfer – executed for the dining room of a resort hotel is specially striking. Another supreme achievement is glass is the massive *verre-églomisé* mural produced by Charles Champigneulle for the French liner *Normandie* to the design of Jean Dupas. The technique involved painting on the reverse side of plate-glass panels, which were then highlighted with gold and silver leaf and finally affixed to a canvas backing. The panels depict the history of navigation in fantastic splendour, complete with a Moses-like Neptune riding on a sea serpent, muscular steeds and mermen, a flock of seagulls and glittering galleons, all floating and flying on a background of stylized waves.

Designers in other countries in the 1920s and 1930s also made significant contributions to glass, in both design and technique. The Swedish firm Orrefors, founded in 1898, received international acclaim at the 1925 Paris Exposition for its beautiful engraved glass vessels, clear or softly tinted. Graal glass, which Orrefors' designer Simon Gate (1883–1945) had developed around 1917 along with glass-blower Knut Bergvist, was similar to Emile Gallé's cameo glass, but its effect was achieved without any kind of relief cutting. Vases, bottles, decanters and other handsome objects were produced in Graal glassware, some decorated with stylized, pneumatic female nudes resembling those in French paintings, others depicting such scenes as a merry bacchanalian romp or country firework displays. More austere, functional glassware was also made by Orrefors in the Art Deco period, designed by, among others, Edvard Hald, Vicke Lindstrand and Edvin Ohrstrøm. The firm continues to make glass today, and indeed Swedish glassmakers have, since the 1920s, been among the leading lights in innovative glass design.

In Finland, the architect-designer Alvar Aalto (1898–1976) also created distinctive glassware in the 1930s. Generally of blown moulded glass with straight sides but oddly shaped, free-flowing perimeters, the vessels were made by the littala company, which still functions today (indeed, some of Aalto's designs remain in production). And in Denmark, the architect-artist Jacob Bang, who was an industrial designer at the Holmegaard glass works from 1925 to 1942, made vessels strongly reminiscent of Maurice Marinot's with simple linear engravings on acid-corroded surfaces.

In the Netherlands, the Leerdam Glasfabrik (the Royal Dutch Glass Works) was founded in 1765, and in the Art Deco period the designer Chris Lebeau made the factory one of the premier European producers of *moderne* glassware. Another designer, Andries Dirk Copier, created exclusive studio glass, known as Unica and Serica, for the firm, as well as goblets and other mass-production tableware. Leerdam also manufactured stained glass, to designs by the Belgian Henri van de Velde, the American Frank Lloyd Wright and Copier, among others.

In Austria, many of the Wiener Werkstätte (Viennese Workshops) designers, including Josef Hoffman, Koloman Moser and Dagobert Peche, were responsible for the production of handsome glassware from 1910 onward. Although these pieces often predate the 1925 Paris Exposition, they are none the less startlingly modern in appearance; typical are the various decanters, tumblers and other tableware made by the Lobmeyr factory and decorated with simple geometric designs or black-enamelled patterns.

Elsewhere in Europe, the Czechoslovakian glass industry – always of major importance in Eastern Europe – produced Art Deco-style glassware, including lamps, vases and tableware, as well as lovely cameo-glass pieces with bold geometric motifs. Art Deco-type glass was produced, to a lesser extent, by Venini of Murano, Italy, which had hitherto made only transitional or revival pieces, reflecting its centuries-old heritage. A second designer, Ercole Barovier, like Venini, also reacted against Venetian revivalism by creating exciting new textures and processes, sometimes decorating simple fluid forms with strong geometric motifs.

English glassware in the Art Deco period was produced by such old, established firms as Thomas Webb and Sons and Stuart and Sons, who hired well-known artists of the fame of Paul Nash, Laura Knight, Eric Ravilious and Graham Sutherland to design glassware for them. But the most highly regarded name in English glass design was Keith Murray, a New Zealand-born architect-designer who had also worked in silver and ceramics. He was a designer first for Whitefriars Glass Works and later for Stevens & Williams, for the second of whom he designed the so-called Brierley Crystal, which had a deeply engraved stylized-cactus motif. Stained glass windows were also produced in abundance for British buildings in the Art Deco period. Notable are those adorned with the ubiquitous sunburst motif, which appeared often on works in various mediums in that largely sun-deprived country. The half-moon design of a stylized sun with projecting rays was not exclusively English, however; it was also used in

*The sensuous draped woman on the left, her back arched and hair a mass of stylized scrolls, is by Gabriel Argy-Rousseau, c.1925–30. The figure is of pâte-de-cristal, which looks more crystalline than pâte-de-verre.*

*The selection of c.1920 Swedish glass, below, shows the range of forms, techniques and motifs found on glassware from the Scandinavian country. The two pieces in the right foreground are examples of Graal glass by the Orrefors firm.*

France and in the United States on everything from enamelled watchcases to sharkskin upholstery.

In the United States, in addition to the Art Nouveau genius Louis Comfort Tiffany, the leading name in glass in the twentieth century was – and still is – the Steuben Glass Works, which Frederick Carder (1864–1963), an Englishman, had founded in Corning, New York, in 1903, and which was taken over by the Corning Glass Works in 1918. Various types of colourful art glass were produced by Steuben during the Art Deco period. In the 1920s Carder added to his output, the *Cintra, Cluthra, Silverine* and *Intarsia* lines, which were mostly vessels made of layers of "cased" glass characterized by internal air bubbles and designs, à la Marinot and other French glassmakers. One handsome Carder piece of the late 1920s, in the shape of a Chinese lotus bowl, and made of frosted glass acid-etched with a stylized flower, constituted more than a passing nod to French glassmaking of the time.

But it was not until the 1920s that Steuben Glass really began to take the lead with its modern wares, which included at least five patterns of elegant, Functionalist crystal stemware designed by Walter Dorwin Teague around 1932. In 1933, Arthur A. Houghton Jr became Steuben's president, and soon afterwards sculptor Sidney B. Waugh was enlisted as a principal designer. Waugh's vases were highly reminiscent of Orrefors', engraved with monumental figures and sleek animals. Many were limited-edition pieces, one of the best known of which was *Gazelle Bowl*, a seven-inch high (17.8cm) engraved-crystal artwork of 1935 decorated with a frieze of these lithe leaping animals which, along with other graceful biches, figured highly in the Art Deco design repertory. Other Waugh bowls depicted mythological characters.

A wide variety of decorative and utilitarian glassware was produced by other American factories, perhaps the most noteworthy being the Ruba Rombic pattern of the Consolidated Lamp and Glass Company of Coraopolis, Pennsylvania (the firm also manufactured designs in the Lalique vein). The mould-blown, non-lead platters, pitchers, candlesticks, goblets, etc, introduced in 1928, were wonderfully geometric, with jagged, jutting-out angles in shades of grey, amber and lavender. The Phoenix Glass Company, also in Pennsylvania, likewise produced both Lalique-style and *moderne* glassware. Much of its output was identical to that of Consolidated, making for many identification problems today.

Among the other American factories, Libbey Glass Company created stunning modern glass, some of which was designed by Walter Dorwin Teague. There were also dozens of lesser companies which multi-mass-produced so-called "Depression" or "Carnival" glass. These were generally imitative, cheaply made coloured pieces which aspired to be art glass, several decades after such glass had gone out of fashion. Among the firms producing Depression glass were A. H. Heisey, Indiana Glass, Anchor Hocking and Fostoria and Federal. Some of these also offered more geometric lines, such as George Sakier's "classic modern" vases of about 1930 for Fostoria.

*Pennsylvania's Consolidated Lamp and Glass Co produced the smoky-grey angular vessels, above, examples of their* Ruba Rombic *pattern. Introduced in 1928, the glass's name derives, according to an advertisement, from "Rubaiy (meaning epic or poem) Rombic (meaning irregular in shape)".*

*René Lalique's massive output included thousands of perfume bottles, including the 11-eyed blue-glass flacon, right, for Canarina. Its design might well have been influenced by kohl-embellished orbs on the faces of Pharaonic Egyptians.*

*The pâte-de-verre glass of Franáois-Emile Décorchement was highly influenced by ancient techniques and motifs. The thick-walled bowl, below, with its mottled orange streaks, has two coiled serpents for handles. The snake derives from Egyptian art and was used by many Art Deco designers.*

*Inexpensive, mass-produced souvenir glass, like the tumbler, above, from the 1939 New York World's Fair, was probably "a dime a dozen" (literally) in the US. The Fair's emblem, the Trylon and Perisphere, can be seen at the far left of the glass.*

Maurice Heaton (b.1900), whose father, the stained glass artist Clement Heaton, emigrated to the United States from Switzerland in about 1910, produced a number of outstanding designs which stand out among American glass of the period. Like Marinot in France, Heaton was a studio artist who metamorphosed simple sheets of bubble-retaining glass into splendid modern abstractions by decorating them with geometric patterns of translucent enamels. Sometimes he would sprinkle powdered glaze over a stencil before firing, thus achieving stunningly patterned plates and bowls. He also designed and executed several large glass murals, including one for the RKO theatre in the Rockefeller Center, which celebrated the solo flight across the Atlantic by Amelia Earhart.

Among stained glass designs in the United States those of Frank Lloyd Wright stand out, including the boldly coloured, almost Mondrian-like windows he created for the Avery Coonley Playhouse in Riverside, Illinois. Many of Wright's stained glass pieces were executed by the Leerdam factory in The Netherlands.

Other decorative, architectural glass was made in great quantities in the United States in the 1920s and 1930s, much of it embellishing shop fronts, restaurants and cinemas, as well as the façades and interiors of Manhattan and Chicago skyscrapers.

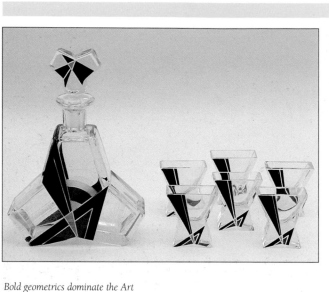

The eight-piece liqueur service, below, was designed by Gabriel Argy-Rousseau, the great French glassmaker whose works were of pâte-de-verre, a type of glass which was not blown, but heated in the mould in a paste mixture. The mottled effect achieved by this technique can best be seen on the handsome tray. The pitcher and tumblers are moulded with an uneven triangle pattern resembling artichoke leaves gone awry.

Bold geometrics dominate the Art Deco cordial set, above, not only in terms of the angular etched- and coloured-enamel decorations, but in the very forms of the decanter and six glasses. Note too how the shape of the decanter's stopper inversely echoes that of its body.

The handsome centrepiece, right, was designed by Walter Dorwin Teague c.1932, for Steuben Glass Works of Corning, NY. Teague was an industrial designer of note who directed his talents to several mediums, including glass. This footed piece, of colourless blown and cut glass, is in the St Tropez pattern, one of a few lines Teague designed for Steuben, the foremost producer of fine American glassware in the Art Deco period.

The shallow bowl, or coupe, right, Trépied Sirène, is by René Lalique, the premier designer of decorative glassware in Art Deco France. The milky blue hue of the solitary sea nymph was achieved in part by adding bits of cobalt to the basic glass mixture. The resultant opalescence highlighted many Lalique pieces, and was widely imitated by others. Note how the siren's hair is made up of long, bubbly strands, and her fins turn into aquatic droplets.

The perfume bottle, or flacon, became an essential accessory on every dressing table by the 1920s. The handsome French example at right, with its concertina base and simple oblong stopper, would have been filled with the owner's favourite scent, or perhaps admired empty.

René Lalique's scent bottles number among the finest of the Art Deco era; he designed bottles empty, for retail sale, as well as models for top parfumeurs, like Coty and D'Orsay. At the far right of the Lalique group, below, are two blue spheres for Worth's scent Dans la Nuit.

Ashtrays became a fashionable table accessory in the 1920s, by which time it had become acceptable for women to smoke in public. The two octagon ashtrays, left, of moulded and frosted glass are by Baccarat. The one at the top depicts a classical nymph blowing what seems to be a pipe; below, a modern woman with marcelled locks puffs on a cigarette.

At left are four bow-tie-shaped perfume bottles by Baccarat, which once held perfume by Guerlain of Paris. The Baccarat firm, near Lunéville, France, was founded in 1765, and continues to produce glass today. In the 1920s and 30s, it was second only to René Lalique in making bottles for a burgeoning perfume industry.

...e stunning black glass inkwell by ...né Lalique, above, is called Biches ...oes); on each side is a scene of deer amid foliage. The graceful woodland creatures were common Art Deco subjects.

The perfume bottle, above, was originally designed by René Lalique around 1929 for Molinard's scent Iles d'Or. Its moulded frieze of classical nudes, continued on the sides and back of the bottle, is highlighted with a golden stain. The design remains in use today, for the perfumes Molinard de Molinard and Habanita.

# FIGURATIVE

The androgynous head, left, Victoire, is one of René Lalique's best-known hood ornaments. The mascot, which has become an icon of Art Deco, is known as Spirit of the Wind in Britain. Seen from this angle, it looks quite horrifying.

The massive blue glass vase, below, is by Daum Frères of Nancy. Its design of stylized tropical birds perched on branches bearing square leaves with dotted centres, is curious.

Marcel Bouraine sculpted the drape-bearing figure, above, c.1928. It was moulded in pâte-de-cristal by Gabriel Argy-Rousseau. The stunning sculpture has Cubist overtones, and the mottled amber glass is truly jewel-like. Bouraine also worked for the Etling firm.

The 17in (42cm) high René Lalique sculpture, left, is called Oiseau de Feu (Firebird). The square base of this stunning c.1925 design could be fitted for electricity to illuminate the top. The feathery hybrid creature occupying the demilune of moulded glass was probably inspired by Stravinsky's Firebird, to which the Ballets Russes danced in Paris.

The pâte-de-verre vase, below, by Gabriel Argy-Rousseau, features a graceful classical dancer in its central panel. The cloudy russet, white and brown vertical designs make a lovely surround. Note the darker hues on the woman's hair, and on the bottom folds of her drapery.

Coq Houdan, left, the brown glass automobile mascot by René Lalique, is a highly angular sculpture, except for the puffed-out breast.

The mascow below, Tête d'Aigle (Eagles Head), is one of René Lalique's most desirable, especially in this light amethyst version.

Gabriel Argy-Rousseau fashioned the pâte-de-cristal vase, below, c.1925. Its pastel palette is unusual for Argy-Rousseau, as is the oriental piscine motif. The waves, crested with pearly dots, are especially lovely.

The Orrefors vase with top, The Negro Hut, right, was designed by Edvard Hald in 1918. Tribal Africa inspired many Art Deco designers, as this lovely blown- and engraved-glass piece shows.

The pâte-de-verre vase, right, is by François-Emile Décorchement, most of whose creations contained evocations of classical Greece and Rome. Note the grape and volute frieze on this piece, as well as the two full-figure "ears". Such varicoloured mottling was also found on ancient

Marius-Ernest Sabino produced La Ronde, *the crystal vase on the right. Unlike René Lalique's more substantial nudes, these four are smooth and supple, and one sports a* severe geometric hairstyle. Sabino was arguably Lalique's closest competitor, although the quality of the latter's output and design was much better and quantity far more numerous.

*e geometric pattern on the pâte- -verre vase is unusually strong for* designer, Gabriel Argy-Rousseau. *e zigzag design on the lower body* the piece has been refined and *ticulated at the top, to become a ck of angled birds in flight. The ndy quality of the moulded glass s been emphasized.*

The monumental figure of Diana moulded on the Steuben Glass bowl, left, stands out. Sidney Waugh designed the piece c.1935 for the Corning, NY, firm. It was inspired in part by Swedish engraved glass, such as the covered vase by Hald to its left. The muscles on the archer and her dog, as on much American sculpture of the time, are exaggerated, especially when compared with the figures on the Scandinavian piece.

*Marcel Goupy enamelled the vase, right, c.1926. Called* Les Baigneuses (The Bathers), *its figures bear no resemblance to those on Cézanne's celebrated earlier canvas of the same name. The use of solid areas of colour – at times outlined by another hue, as on the bodies and water – is a striking device. Goupy also designed porcelain tableware for Haviland at Limoges.*

# ORGANIC MOTIFS

The jewel-like vase, below, was designed in the 1920s by Frederick Carder, head of Steuben Glass. Its floral motif harks back to the American firm's earlier Art Nouveau glass, but its hexagonal shape and brilliant hue are decidedly moderne.

Languedoc, right, is one of René Lalique's most striking vases, especially in this rich shade of green. Its overall design comprises the prickly leaf-ends of the Sansevieria plant, but is so stylized as to create a near-abstract pattern.

Steuben's Frederick Carder designed the lily vase, above, part of the firm's Ivrene line. The vase seems to shimmer with pearly iridescence.

The Parisian Marcel Goupy designed and enamelled this blown-glass vase c.1925. Goupy, who also worked in ceramics, "painted" his glassware wit distinctive floral and figural designs, sometimes both inside and out.

abriel Argy-Rousseau designed the
unning pâte-de-verre vase below.
While studying ceramics at Sèvres,
the designer began to experiment with
pâte-de-verre. He soon devoted
himself fully to this newly revived
technique of glass-making, first
exhibiting his work in 1914.

The floral-design glass bowl, right, by
Quenvit, was hand-painted with
enamels. The gold-yellow-black
palette was one common to Quenvit,
whose glass pieces also often featured
metal mounts or bases.

The mottled blue-black vase, left, is
by Daum Frères, a Nancy, France,
firm founded in 1889 by the brothers
Auguste and Antonin Daum. The
factory's initial output was in the
organic and curvilinear Art Nouveau
style, but by the 1920s their pieces
became more stylized and geometric.
The chief design on this vase is that of
a thorny branch, which resembles the
pattern on René Lalique's
Tourbillons vase (see page 87).

# GEOMETRIC

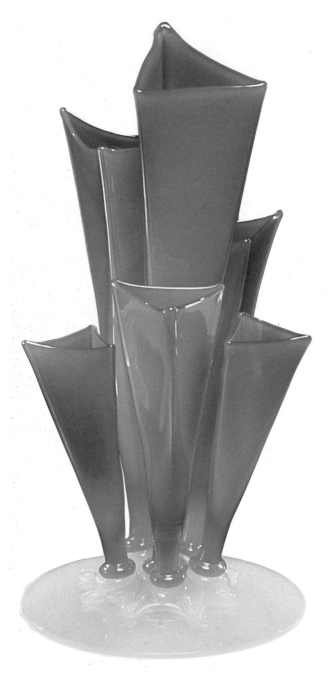

The 1925 vase, below, is Czechoslovak, probably by Wondřejc. The clear- and cut-glass piece is a bold yet simple design, with thick walls and sharp angles. Czechoslovakia, especially that part of the country encompassing old Bohemia, has long been a producer of decorative glass.

Antonin Daum of Daum Frères designed the bottle, above, c.1929. The vessel is of thick, gold-flecked glass, which has been cased with a layer of clear glass. The top layer has in turn been acid-etched with an unruly geometric design.

The vase, left, was designed by Jean Luce around 1927–28. It has been sand-blasted with a geometric pattern, creating a patchwork surface of rough and smooth textures. Luce designed porcelain and glass tableware for the ocean liner Normandie.

Frederick Carder of Steuben Glass designed the prong vase above, c.1930. The jade-green "stems" are attached to an alabaster-glass base. Although a plant-like form, the striking multi-part vase is above all a geometric configuration – and one quite revolutionary for Carder, most of whose Art Deco-era creations retained Art Nouveau-style designs.

The liqueur set, above, dates from the 1920s and is possibly by the French firm, Baccarat. The black-enamel decoration on the angled tumblers (whose inner bowls are perfectly round) is irregular, and quite different from the sunburst motif on the decanter.

The René Lalique vase, left, is called Tourbillons (Whirlwinds), and it was available in colours as well as black-enamelled colourless glass. A similar example was exhibited at the 1925 Paris Exposition. Although it appears monumental in size, the vase is only 8in (20.4cm) high. The prickly vortical design is moulded in high relief on a thick body.

The English talcum-powder bottle, above, sports a quarter-sunburst pattern. The ubiquitous rayed motif – whether partial, half or whole – was found on glass of all sorts, especially in Britain and the United States.

# TECHNIQUES

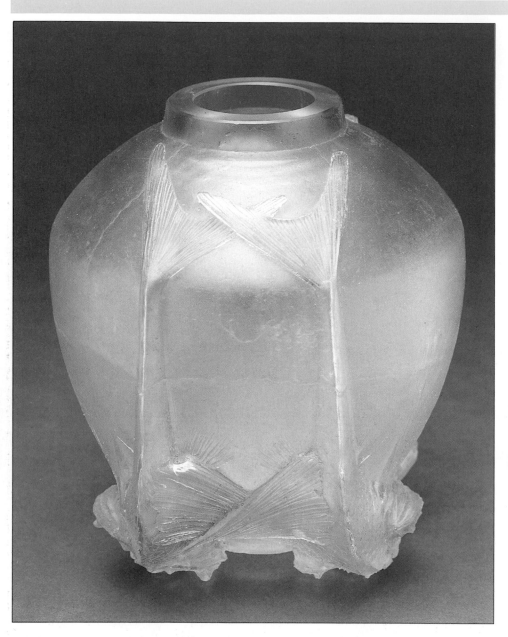

Lalique designed the above cire-perdue glass vase in 1923. This "lost wax" method was adapted from bronze-casting: a model is carved in wax and a clay mixture is allowed to harden around it. The wax is then melted out and replaced by molten glass. Finally, the clay mould is broken up to reveal the glass sculpture within.

The elaborate vase on stand, right, was designed by the Frenchman Auguste Heiligenstein. Gilt and enamel adorn the vase, which depicts dancing classical figures at top, a geometric pattern below. Heiligenstein first executed enamelled designs for Marcel Goupy, later worked in both glass and ceramics.

he 1920s vase, left, has a blown-
ass centre by Daum and wrought-
on mount by Majorelle. The
ottling on the glass and the
eometric design of the metal are in
ark contrast to earlier works by
ese French firms, whose greatest
me was in the Art Nouveau period.

The rich internal decorations on the
flask, right, are unmistakably
Maurice Marinot. Note how the tiny
button stopper is the same green hue
as streaks within the flak's body.

he above blown-glass vase comes
om Murano, the famed Venetian
lass centre. A stylized harvest scene
as been applied to the rich plum-
oloured body in strokes of black and
old.

The flask and stopper, right, was
hand-blown and acid-etched by
Maurice Marinot in 1929. Many of
his works were internally decorated
with air bubbles or chemical
inclusions; within this piece float tiny
black particles.

## MAURICE MARINOT

Maurice Marinot
(1882–1960) began his
artistic career as a painter, a
member of the radical Fauve
brotherhood. He also ended
his working life with brush in
hand, but from the years
1911 to 1937, he devoted
himself to the creation of
hand-blown glass vessels, all
brought about quite
serendipitously by a visit to a
friend's glass factory in Bar-
sur-Seine. He became
enamoured of the mercurial
material which started out a
mass of chemicals, evolved
into a molten liquid and,
finally, emerged a solid jewel.
He apprenticed himself to
some gaffers, or glass-
blowers, worked hard at
learning his new craft (he
enamelled pieces at first, then
actually blew the glass), and
by 1922 was exhibiting his
works – to great acclaim.
Unlike René Lalique, the bulk
of whose glass was mass
produced, Marinot
singlehandedly created jars,
vases, *flacons* and the like –
some 2,500 in all, in simple
shapes which fit into the Art
Deco repertory. What made
his pieces special, however,
were the decorations he
added to them – chemical
streaks, patterned air bubbles,
etc – as well as the acid baths
he subjected them to, and the
several layers of glass he
sometimes built them up
out of.

The above panels, showing the top of a golden galleon, were once part of a huge glass mural in the Grand Salon of the French ocean liner, Normandie. A "floating palace of Art Deco', the ship contained many noted French artists' works, including this fantastic history-of-navigation mural, conceived by Jean Dupas and executed by Charles Champigneulle in verré-eglomisé, a technique which involves painting on the reverse side of plate-glass panels.

A great deal of decorative architectural glass was made in the 1930s in the United States, to be integrated into the tall buildings which began to define the skylines of many a growing metropolis. The sculptural glass panel, left, was designed by the architectural firm Shreve, Lamb & Harmon and executed by Steuben Glass of Corning, NY. The architects were responsible for, among others, the design of the colossal Empire State Building in Manhattan.

e ubiquitous Art Deco glassmaker,
né Lalique, designed large-scale
chitectural pieces as well as
pleware. The 9ft (2.7m) high glass
nel, below, depicts a classical male
de in a leafy surround. Lalique
signed it in 1932 for John
anamaker's Philadelphia
partment store, one of several
merican commissions be received.

Some outstanding stained glass pieces
were made in France in the Art Deco
period, including windows and panels
by Jacques Gruber, who earlier
created nature-inspired works in the
Art Nouveau style. The example on
the right, however, is pure Art Deco.
The window was one of a series of
sports players Gruber executed for
the dining room of a resort hotel.

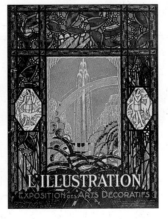

In June 1925, the cover of
L'Illustration magazine featured a
rendering of the stained glass work of
Gaétan Jeannin. The piece, Le Jet
d'Eau (Water Jet), was displayed at
the Pavillon des Vitraux (Stained
Glass Window Pavilion) at the
Paris Exposition. The design is rich in
stylized floral and figural decoration,
which was typical of the Art Deco
period.

*Summer rug by the Waite Carpet Company, US, c.1929*

# CHAPTER • FIVE

# CARPETS, TEXTILES AND LIGHTING

The Art Deco period witnessed a profusion of decorative lighting devices, the inevitable result of the fairly recent discovery of electricity. They were sometimes adorned extravagantly in colourful, showy garb, sometimes more restrained – mostly in the United States – in streamlined, *moderne* dress. Lamps of all shapes and sizes – table and floor models, sconces and chandeliers – appeared in the modern interior, often as a subtle, subdued element, but at other times (as during the Art Nouveau period) as a highly visible, significant *objet d'art* or piece of furniture.

It was the French who created the widest range of decorative lighting devices. The glassmakers René Lalique, Daum Frères and Gabriel Argy-Rousseau, the metalworker Edgar Brandt, and numerous sculptors and furniture designers – Pierre Legrain, Pierre Chareau, Desny, Armand-Albert Rateau, Jean Goulden, Eileen Gray, Jean Lambert-Rucki among others – applied their creative skills to this new marriage of science and art. They designed glorious night lights, standard lamps, ceiling lights and chandeliers.

Jean Perzel, a designer who had studied painting and glassmaking in Munich and settled in Paris in 1910, specialized in lighting, not only creating wonderfully geometric shades, sconces, ceiling lamps and such, but also sensitively relating these objects and the light they emitted to their environment. His lamps, often of brass with frosted white or pink glass, had strong yet subtle angular forms; they were similar to those of Desny, devoid of the ornamentation which characterized other lamps of the period.

Foremost among the ornate lighting devices are the standard lamps of Armand-Albert Rateau and Edgar Brandt. One of Rateau's, made of green-patinated bronze, had tripod feet of birds echoed by a frame of avian heads which held the bulb at the top. Brandt's example, also of bronze, was in the shape of a tall, coiling cobra in whose neck nestled an etched-glass bowl by Daun.

Jean Goulden's table lamps, usually of silvered metal and enamel, were quite sculptural and Cubist, while those of Jean Lambert-Rucki, although often also carved and sculptural, paid homage to tribal Africa with their stylized figures. Eileen Gray designed several lamps, including a standing model in lacquered wood with a parchment shade which she created for the 1923 *Salon des Artistes Décorateurs*. Both base and shade sport numerous jutting triangles and angles, making the creation both highly futuristic and extremely whimsical.

The lighting devices of René Lalique ran the gamut from sculptures to table lamps with beautiful crescent-shaped tops, and to ceiling, wall lights and chandeliers, with floral and geometric motifs. Even his automobile mascots could be fitted to light up. His *Grand boulle de gui* (literally, a large ball of mistletoe) comprised 10 pieces of convex glass moulded with a mistletoe design and attached to each other with metal rings to form a massive sphere.

*The brass and cut-crystal chandelier, below, is Czech designed in 1913 by Josef Gočár (who created that country's pavilion at the 1925 Paris Exposition). It is an unusual example of Czech Cubism, which embraced objects as well as fine arts.*

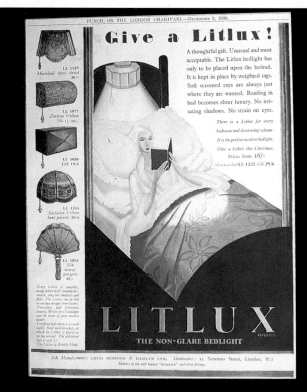

*The bronze floor lamp, above, is a chic Art Deco design, with its steppe[d] base and top, and geometric shade. Notice the stem's two jagged sections resembling a broken-off stem.*

*The 1930 advertisement from Punc[h] left, for Litlux lamps offers the bedtime reader a wide variety of contemporary lights to attach to the headboard. The fluted model over th[e] woman's head is especially modern[e].*

*ne so-called "Silver Entrance" of ondon's Park Lane Hotel, above, atures stunning lighting fixtures om 1927, the year the hotel opened. ne corner lights on the balustrades e striking with their openwork matures.*

simple and understated, some sculptural and Cubist – were undeniably handsome and distinctive, contributing one more significant dimension to a functional item.

As in other disciplines, Parisian textiles, carpets and wall hangings of the 1920s and 1930s were highly innovative and influential. But the designs of England and the United States excelled as well, and there was much interchange between these and other western countries – not to the mention the fact that a number of women were making their mark in virtually all of them.

The tradition of carpet-making is an old and respected one in France, and the Art Deco period witnessed not only a proliferation of rugs in different shapes and sizes, but also an increase in their significance in terms of overall interior design. Numerous *ensembliers* (see the section on furniture) designed carpets, including Emile-Jacques Ruhlmann, René Herbst, Robert Mallet-Stevens, Eugène Printz and Eileen Gray. Many artists too applied their talents to rug design, among them the painters Marie Laurencin and Fernand Léger and the sculptor Gustave Miklos.

The greatest French rug designer of them all, however, was Ivan da Silva Bruhns, whose deeply coloured, geometric creations mirrored much of the fine art of the period, ie Cubist and Constructivist, as indeed did many other rug designs. They also took their inspiration from deep-wool Berber carpets often in red and black, fine examples of which had been seen at exhibitions of Moroccan art in Paris in 1917, 1919 and 1923. Similar carpets were designed by Jean Lurçat, Henri Stéphany, Louis Marcoussis, Sonia Delaunay, Eileen Gray and Evelyn Wyld, the last two British expatriates who lived in Paris. Eileen Gray's rugs were especially innovative and witty; one, her *Blackboard* of 1923, is in production again today.

Other Parisian designers created carpets with Fauve-like colours, which were often round and prettier in concept, with floral designs. Edouard Bénédictus, Paul Follot, André Groult, Süe et Mare, Maurice Dufrêne, and the Ateliers Martine, Pomone and Primavera were some of the exponents of this more decorative school. Marie Laurencin produced a scallop-edged round carpet with mermaids, fish and doves in pastel shades of pink and blue, and many of Bénédictus's huge rugs were awash with bright floral patterns.

In England, two carpet designers of note emerged, E. McKnight Kauffer and his wife Marion Dorn; both were American-born, and collaborated on modernist rugs for Wilton Royal, as well as designing on their own. McKnight Kauffer's rugs were quite painterly, comprising stripes and blocks of pure colour, sometimes overlapping, while Marion Dorn's were more sensitive to the medium, often employing cut pile to attain layered effects. Her designs were also less rectilinear than her husband's, featuring interlocking loop patterns, sometimes symmetrical, sometimes free-flowing, as well as tiers of zigzags. And her colours were rather earthy – beiges, browns, greys – as opposed to his more vivid, even off-beat, hues and combinations. The team influenced

Perhaps the most popular lamps were the small table models, produced by Daum Frères and Schneider/Le Verre Français among others. They usually had mushroom-shaped shades topping round, cylindrical or oval vases and were made of either white or coloured glass with etched geometric motifs. In addition to the well-known French firms who turned out these decorative and practical pieces, there were numerous anonymous companies – French, Dutch, Czechoslovakian, German – who marketed them. The Bauhaus also designed functional lighting devices, including Marianne Brandt's revolutionary Kandem bedside lamp of 1928, which was the basis for many lamps in wide use today.

In the United States, many industrial designers directed their talents to lighting fixtures, among them Walter von Nessen, Raymond Loewy and Walter Dorwin Teague. Furniture/interior designers, such as Donald Deskey, Kem Weber and Gilbert Rohde also produced table and standard lamps, or *torchères*, as did Frank Lloyd Wright. On the whole, American lamps were ultra-modern, streamlined and/or geometric, composed of contemporary materials – Bakelite, Lucite, Formica, steel, brushed chromium and aluminium. Often reminiscent of Jean Perzel's Parisian output, they tended to be primarily lighting devices – and "decorative' only secondarily. None the less, their shapes – some such other English designers as Ronald Grierson, Ian Henderson and Marian Pepler. Betty Joel, the furniture designer, also created rugs, in effect becoming the English near-equivalent of a Parisian *ensemblier*. The Omega Workshops had also produced rugs earlier, including one of about 1913 by Vanessa Bell, with an abstract pattern of intersecting lines which could well have been made 20 years later by Marion Dorn or Marian Pepler.

In other European countries, such as Austria, Sweden and Germany, modernist designs appeared on many hand-woven and machine-made rugs, but traditional folkart patterns were employed as well. Bruno Paul and Ernest Boehm were two talented German designers whose products were either geometric or floral, with muted shades and interesting plays of light and dark.

American rugs were influenced largely by the geometric arm of French rug design, with such talents as Donald Deskey, Gilbert Rohde, Eugene Schoen, Ruth Reeves and Loja Saarinen making significant contributions. Deskey's designs, although usually geometric, often approached abstraction. He created carpeting for Radio City Music Hall in New York, for instance, composed of an abstract pattern of jazz musicians with their instruments. Ruth Reeves was also responsible for a bold and colourful design, her *Electric* rug of 1930, which was decorated with a zigzag lightning-bolt pattern in red, green and blue; this was a firm, modern statement suited to its intended use in a family radio room. Some of the handsomest Art Deco American carpet designs, however, were anonymous; these included a variety of geometric-patterned rugs made by the huge Bigelow Hartford and W. & J. Sloane Manufacturing companies.

**M**any of the same Parisians who designed carpets also worked on textiles and fabrics. There were, in addition, a number of other extremely talented practitioners, among them Robert Bonfils, Francis Jourdain, Hélène Henry, Paul Poiret and, the most famous of all, Raoul Dufy, who designed charming and colourful tapestry upholstery, screens, wall hangings and the like, which were produced by Gobelins, Aubusson and Beauvais.

Hélène Henry's silk and rayon fabrics were notable for their thick, "natural" textiles, in appropriate earthy tones of yellow, grey and brown. Her motifs were usually geometric, but far subtler than the rather "loud" arcs and angles of Maurice Dufràne, Sonia Delaunay and the Burkhalter and Valmier fabric houses.

Designs on fabrics and upholstery were generally more pictorial and painterly than those on carpets. Dufy presented elaborate scenes of well-dressed ladies at horse races (a frequent watercolour subject of his), as well as densely packed panoramas of fishermen, harvesters and dancers. These last were made in cotton by Bianchini-Férier, most often in black and white, but sometimes also in yellow and white or red and white. Léger and Jourdain designed in more abstract and geometric terms, as did Ruhlmann, who created large, bold, circular patterns for furniture covering, which were quite innovative and repeated by many

*Sonia Delaunay's* Simultané *shantung fabric, right, is in a bright, geometric pattern as were most of the Russian-born woman's designs. Delaunay also created smart sportswear and accessories in collaboration with couturier Jacques Heim*

*The carpet, above, was designed c.1926 by Louis Marcoussis for the studio of couturier Jacques Doucet. The Polish-born Marcoussis, a friend of Braque, Picasso and Apollinaire, was also a noted printmaker.*

*Paris's best-known carpet designer, Ivan da Silva Bruhns, created the wool rug, right, c.1932. Many of Bruhns' designs were inspired by deep-wool Berber carpets.*

*...e woven fabric sample, above, ...rs a rich repeating pattern in ...ck and plum. Probably of ...merican origin, the design is both ...rid and geometric.*

Although textile design in the United States was influenced by France, the results were usually simpler in both motif and hue. Ruth Reeves, a major figure in American textiles, designed wall hangings, rugs and fabrics which were joyfully *moderne* and undeniably American, with names like *American Scene, Manhattan*, and *Homage to Emily Dickinson*. She studied with Léger in Paris and her painterly wall hanging, *Figures with Still Life*, is much indebted to his work. Others of her patterns are more light-hearted, showing cosy domestic scenes or New York tourist attractions. Her colours were often quite subdued – browns, greens, black – allowing the strong patterns to predominate.

Colours and motifs were more equally balanced in the work of the Karasz sisters, Ilonka and Mariska – the former, the designer, the latter, the producer – who emigrated to the United States from Hungary in 1913. Abstract floral designs in bright colours characterized their handworked pieces, with more than a passing nod to their Eastern European heritage. The "silk murals", as she termed them, of Lydia Bush-Brown were more pictorial, usually incorporating stylized borders, often inspired by oriental or Middle Eastern subjects. Some, however, were quite American, such as a silk batik hanging called *Manhattan*, which has a border of bridges, skyscrapers and oil tanks.

The patterns of many of the French and American designers were also used for wallpaper. Ruth Reeves, Raoul Dufy and Donald Deskey were among those whose creations could be found covering just about every element in a room – wallpaper, rugs, curtains, upholstery. Since the techniques used to reproduce designs on paper were similar to those for cloth, the crossover from one medium to the other was almost effortless for the designers. Interestingly enough, Le Corbusier abhorred the use of patterned wallpaper or any other kind of wall covering, advocating instead white-painted walls (which would indeed become the norm by the 1930s).

other designers; these often had floral or foliate motifs which echoed those appearing on some of the furniture of the period. Jean Lurçat's tapestry designs could be busily pictorial, but some were restrained and appropriate to upholstery – a sofa covering, for instance, imitating fringed valances.

In England, Marion Dorn, Vanessa Bell, Duncan Grant, the partnership of Phyllis Barron and Dorothy Larcher, Alec Hunter, Nancy Ellis, Enid Marx, Norman Webb, Gregory Brown, Frank Dobson, Minnie McLeish and Charles Rennie Mackintosh among many others, designed fabrics and textiles. Most tended towards distinctive *moderne* patterns which featured stylized flowers, birds and human figures, as well as abstract and rigidly geometric designs. In Russia, Varvara and Stepanova and Liubov Popova created brightly hued fabrics and textiles grounded on the circle and the square. Russian-born Sonia Delaunay and Swiss-born Sophie Taeuber-Arp, who were both Paris-based, devised textiles in vivid colours and, again, in abstract designs. Indeed, nowhere more than in tapestries and textiles did the fine arts make so great an impact in the 1920s and 1930s, with painterly patterns translated into cloth and yarn.

In Germany, the Bauhaus weaving workshop produced carpets, woollen wall hangings and fabrics in strong shades, usually in geometric or abstract patterns. Their emphasis was often on texture, and they employed an extensive range of fabrics. Gunta Stölzl and Anni Albers, two of their most influential figures, eventually settled respectively in Switzerland and the United States.

The wall lamp, left, is from the Burnt Oak Savoy, London (now a Top Rank Club). The fountain-like motif was adapted from Parisian design.

German-born industrial designer Walter von Nessen, who opened a New York studio c.1925, created the aluminium, glass and Bakelite lamp, right. Unlike his earlier, more decorative devices, this model is a crisp and functional product of the Machine Age.

The multi-bulbed ceiling fixture, right, is featured at the Liverpool Forum (today a Cannon cinema). Its starburst-and-chevron design, alternating with eight leafy rays, is a prime example of the flamboyant lighting devices that adorned many theatres in the Art Deco era, both in the United States and United Kingdom.

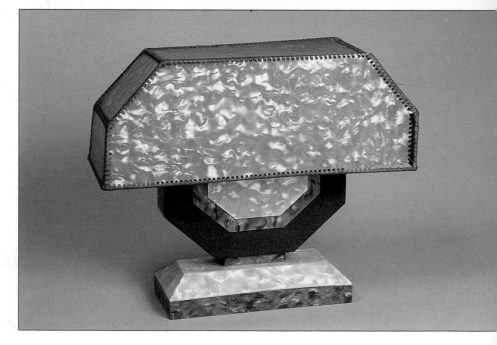

The plastic table lamp, right, comprises several pieces, in tones of cream and russet, which have been either fused together or sewn at the joint. The overall geometrics combine to create a smart – and at the time, inexpensive – 1920s accessory.

The 1920s table lamp, left, is sheathed with mottled plastic, in two shades simulating tortoiseshell and born. The chalice-like design, quite sophisticated for such an everyday object, is reminiscent of early Australian pieces.

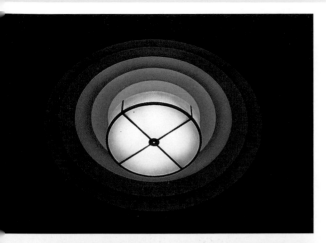

The handsome ceiling light, left, illuminates the circle of the Esher Embassy theatre, Surrey. Its fixture's design of concentric circles in hues of red encloses a circular shade in a simple wrought-metal armature.

Emile-Jacques Ruhlmann, the Parisian ensemblier known best for his furniture, designed the lighting sconce, left. The alabaster shade, with its subtle striations, is perched on a smart metal mount, its top dotted with silvery beads, its bottom gently fluted.

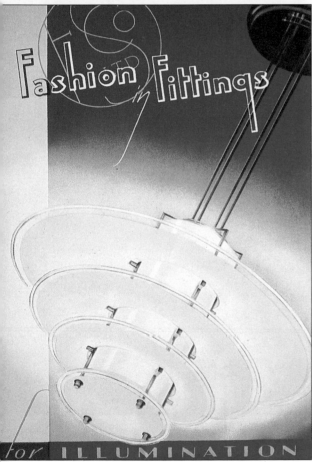

he advertisement for a British ghting firm, above, illustrates a oderne chandelier whose design of oncentric circles is not unlike that of e lamp featured above.

Daum Frères designed the table lamp, right, its base and matching creamy shade of glass decorated with vertical ribs and squares on a rough, granular surface.

# FANTASY

New Yorker Arthur von Frankenberg created the table lamp, below, sold through Frankart, Inc, whose products took their inspiration from luxurious French designs, but were cheaply cast in inexpensive metals.

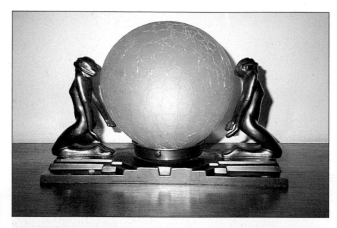

The trio of bronze nudes, left, their toes touching a glass base, hold up a two-part, fountain-like glass shade. The designer of this 1920s lamp was the versatile Frederic Carder, founder of Steuben Glass in Corning, New York.

The great Parisian ironworker, Edgar Brandt, designed the elaborate wall sconce, above. The somewhat roughly formed leaves and tendrils are contrasted with the septet of stylized blossoms, their petals gently scrolling in one expertly executed piece.

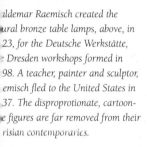

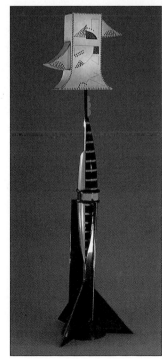

ldemar Raemisch created the
ural bronze table lamps, above, in
23, for the Deutsche Werkstätte,
 Dresden workshops formed in
98. A teacher, painter and sculptor,
emisch fled to the United States in
37. The disproprotionate, cartoon-
 figures are far removed from their
risian contemporaries.

 lacquered-wood and painted-
rchment floor lamp, right, is by the
sh-born Eileen Gray, who produced
-seeing designs for buildings,
ects and interiors during her long
eer. The lamp was featured in a
droom-boudoir for Monte Carlo",
ich she displayed at the 14th Salon
s Artistes Décorateurs in Paris.

The striding rooster, above, is in fact a
lamp, with a bulb cleverly concealed
in its orange glass body, which has
been blown into an iron armature.
This is the product of Müller Frères of
Lunéville, France, established in
1895. Three of the Müller brothers
had once worked for the Art Nouveau
glassmaker Emile Gallé.

René Lalique's immense glass oeuvre
included a variety of lighting devices,
some of the most beautiful being the
tiara veilleuse type of lamp, with
overflowing "stoppers" like those on
perfume bottles. The example, left,
features two full-feathered peacocks
topping a frosted glass base with a
fluted cylindrical shape.

# GEOMETRIC

The " Paisley " Decoration.
Novel stiling treatment and modern corner motifs.

Russian-born Sonia Delaunay produced the watercolour, left, called Simultané (Simultaneous). The colourful fabric design is typical of the artist's output, with its painterly composition and bold geometrics.

The wool rug, below, is by Ivan da Silva Bruhns. His geometric creations reflected Cubist and Constructivist art, but were also inspired by deep wool Berber carpets. The example shown, c.1930, was made for the Maharajah of Indore, an important patron of the time.

Despite its name, The Paisley Decoration, the illustration, top, from a British advertisement of 1935, features a stylish moderne wallpaper border, with a corner cluster of bright diagonals.

The corner design, directly above, from a 1930s British wallpaper sample, comprises a smart rectilinear pattern, a variation on the sunray motif so prevalent in the 1930s, especially in Britain.

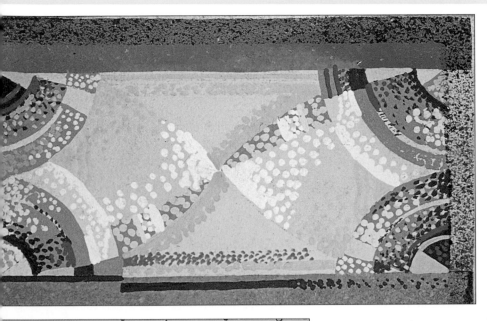

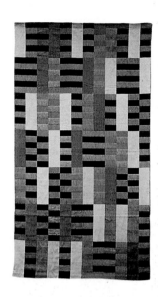

*Eric Bagge's carpet, Arc-en-Ciel (Rainbow), produced by Lucien-Boux, c.1926. Bagge was a French architect interior decorator.*

*The Bauhaus designer Anni Albers created the triple-weave wall-hanging, right, c.1925.*

*British designer Marian Pepler's 1933 drawing for her hand-tufted Peru rug appears at left. Its soft, muted colours were made popular by another female carpet designer in Britain, Marion Dorn.*

*At right is an example of Hélène Henry's fabric designs, c.1925. The self-taught Parisian's silk and rayon materials were noted for their thick, "natural" look and their neutral hues.*

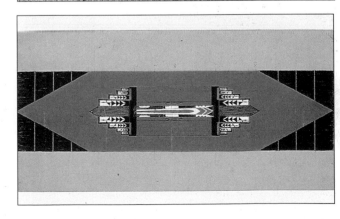

*Hungarian-born painter/sculptor/designer Gustave Miklos drew the carpet design, right, in 1921. It was probably one of the several rugs he designed for his patron, couturier Jacques Doucet. Its red and black central motif bears a close resemblance to some of his abstract Cubist sculptures.*

# MOTIFS

The wall-hanging, left, is by Marianne Geyer-Pankok. The 1921 tapestry is a vibrant example of that arm of Eastern European crafts of the 1920s and 1930s which was largely influenced by traditional peasant art.

Interior decorator Maurice Dufrène designed the carpet, below, in 1922. Its all-over floral motif is found on many Art Deco floor coverings. From 1921 Dufrène was in charge of the Galleries Lafayette's workshop, La Maîtrise.

The wallpaper design, above, called Nicotine, is from the second-mezzanine men's smoking room at Radio City Music Hall, part of Manhattan's Rockefeller Center (1931–40). The talented Donald Deskey, who oversaw the decoration of Radio City, designed the wall covering, which is printed in cocoa brown on golden-foil paper. Note the masculine "toys", including cigars, playing cards, dice and boats, depicted rather incongruously with dark-skinned tobacco-field workers.

« NOUVELLES VARIATIONS » par BÉNÉDICTUS.                    Pl. 17

The British wallpaper border, below, with its combination floral-geometric design, is related to the Bénédictus pattern to its left. The blossoms too are reminiscent of those painted on Clarice Cliff's crocus-pattern tableware.

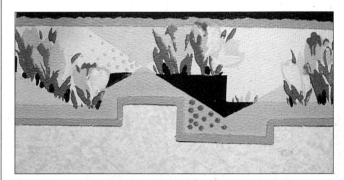

Édouard Bénédictus was a foremost designer of floral fabrics and carpets in Art Deco Paris; one of his rich gouache designs is shown above, along with two small landscapes. The strong geometrics of the top drawing are rather unusual for Bénédictus, whose albums of textile patterns were widely used by other Art Deco designers. The plate shown is from the album Nouvelles Variations.

The 1925–30 fabric design, right, is by Robert Bonfils, known for bookbindings and graphics, as well as lushly patterned cottons and silks, some of which were made by the firm Bianchini-Férier. The cross-hatching on the water-lily pattern gives it a strong graphic quality.

The golden tropical motif on the roundel, above, would no doubt have brightened up the corner of a 1930s sitting-room interior. The design features on an otherwise plain, sandy-textured British wallpaper pattern.

The Art Deco headscarf, above, is covered with a racing-car motif. One can imagine it having been tied under the chin of an adventurous lady taking a spin in a 1930s open-top automobile. The scarf is reminiscent of contemporaneous paintings, with its bright colours and cartoon-like drawing.

# MOTIFS

The painter and illustrator Raoul
…fy designed the fabric, right, in
…25. He also designed tapestries and
…ll-hangings, most of them as
…ctorial as his works on canvas. The
…ample pictured was probably
…eated for Bianchini-Férier, for
…om he worked until 1930; before
…t he was employed by Paul Poiret,
…o established a design studio for
…e young artist.

…e gifted all-round designer, Maurice
…ufrène, created the handsome
…bric, below, around 1925–30. He
…gan his career at the turn of the
…ntury, and, interestingly, the Art
…eco-era fabric illustrated bears
…stiges of the earlier curvilinear and
…ganic style known as Art Nouveau.

The printed-cloth design, below, was
manufactured by Bianchini-Férier in
1920, after a design by Raoul Dufy.
Called La Moisson (The Harvest)
and part of the Toiles de Tournon
line, the complex, painterly design
was also available in red on white and
black on white.

The above silk headscarf, shot through
with silver threads and comprising a
dazzling display of flowers and
zigzags, is probably French. Such
stylized blossoms, however, coupled
with geometric elements, could be
found on fabric woven, embroidered
and printed throughout Europe and
North America.

*The Chrysler Building, New York City, 1930 (William van Alen, architect)*

# CHAPTER • SIX

# ARCHITECTURE

Art Deco architecture, unlike other areas of Art Deco design, was dominated not by the French but by the Americans. Although most of the buildings created for the 1925 Paris Exposition were of course Art Deco by their very nature, they were only temporary and thus ephemeral. Later designers and architects know them only through photographs and drawings, but purists argue that they represent history's only true Art Deco architecture. The buildings that have come so gloriously to epitomize Art Deco – or, more appropriately, Modernism – are still very much in evidence today, scraping the skies of New York, Chicago and other American cities with their pointed turrets, stepped elevations, decorative finials and geometric friezes. Less lofty structures, too – cinemas, department stores, hotels, private homes – contain elements of Art Deco; examples abound in the United States, Britain, Germany, France and wherever else the design principles of Le Corbusier and the Bauhaus school, and the design elements of high-style French Art Deco, were adopted or adapted.

The 1925 Paris Exposition was, despite its transitoriness, the premier showcase for Art Deco architecture. Although many of the structures bore vestiges of an earlier monumental style dating from about 1900, several pavilions were strongly modernist, some in overall design, but most in terms of such added elements as gates by Edgar Brandt, stylized figural bas-reliefs or floral and geometric embellishments. Although they were not created to be practical, they were in themselves excellent show pieces. Robert Mallet-Stevens' *Pavillon du Tourisme*, for instance, was a handsome rectilinear building with a numberless – indeed faceless – clock topping a cruciform tower.

The pavilions of the four Parisian department stores, the Louvre, Au Bon Marché, Au Printemps and Galeries Lafayette, were all stunning Art Deco designs. Au Bon Marché's, created by Louis Boileau, was a squat, squarish, stepped building, gloriously dominated by a leaded-glass panel at the entrance, which was alive with arcs, zigzags and other geometric shapes; these were echoed on the stairway, in the ironwork and on the bas-relief cement cladding. Galeries Lafayette's was even more dramatic, with a long flight of steps leading to a doorway topped by a massive Jacques Gruber sunburst panel in leaded glass; this was framed by four columns surmounted by figures symbolizing feather, fur, lace and ribbon.

Without doubt, the most striking structure at the Exposition, and the most controversial in terms of its then-and-future significance, was Le Corbusier's *L'Esprit Nouveau* pavilion. Stripped of what he considered abhorrent decorative art – "a dying thing," he termed it – it was instead filled with mass-produced standardized objects. The furnishings were rather boring and awkward, but the structure itself lived up to its title, *The New Spirit* – flooded with light and high ceilinged, its rooms and spaces practically designed.

Others were working along the same modernist, functional lines, among them Robert Mallet-Stevens, Gabriel Guévrékian,

*Although never intended to be permanent, the pavilions and other structures at the 1925 Paris Exposition have had a lasting impact on architects and designers. On the right is a view of the* Porte d'Honneur *entrance to the Fair, featuring Edgar Brandt's ornamental metalwork.*

*On America's West Coast, many sparkling-white Art Deco structures were built along palm-lined streets. The Los Angeles edifice, above, massive and temple-like, is awash with Art Deco elements: floral capitals, neo-classical urns, stepped sections, and simple lines and circles*

# ARCHITECTURE

One great Manhattan skyscraper is the stepped Chanin Building (Sloan & Robertson, 1929). The brochure issued by Irwin S. Chanin, left, was a handsome promotional effort which no doubt helped fill its offices. It features an ethereal portrait of the impressive structure and a detail of one of the decorative lobby grilles.

1930s cinemas were often arresting architectural designs, appropriate to the fantasy worlds they offered behind their doors. Below is a detail of the towering white mass of the Weston-super-Mare Odeon (T. Cecil Howitt, 1935).

Djo-Bourgeois, André Lurçat and Eileen Gray in France, as well as Walter Gropius and Mies van der Rohe in Germany and such architects as Walter Reitz and Adolf Rading elsewhere in northern Europe. In the United States, Frank Lloyd Wright was designing houses that complemented, rather than imposed upon, their natural setting. They were fine examples of practical domestic architecture, made largely of wood and glass materials which integrated themselves better into their often wood surroundings than did the stark-white finishes of Gropius Mallet-Stevens and Eileen Gray.

An interesting architectural sideline here is the white-washed, pastel-highlighted architecture of Old Miami Beach, Florida, much of it featuring combinations of curved and flat walls, circular or polygonal windows offset by rectilinear frames, cantilevered sections and profuse metal railings, often "bent" – all of which could be found on Modernist structures by the likes of Le Corbusier and the Bauhaus figures. But Miami's architects – about whom little is known except their names, Albert Anis, L. Murray Dixon and Henry Hohauser among them – also incorporated unmistakable tropical elements, such as jalousied windows, marine motifs, and daubs, stripes and even huge block of colours, into their structures, with some hotels and houses taking on distinctly nautical looks, portholes and all. Stylized flowers and leaves and geometric designs were found in relief on concrete overdoor panels and in wrought-iron on gates, fences and doors. All in all, these delightful buildings took the pragmatism of modern architecture and coupled it with the romance and fantasy of holiday living – resulting in a unique urban district – which is thankfully well preserved for enthusiastic visitors today.

The most complete expression of Art Deco architecture is, of course, the skyscraper, that symbol of success, industry and capitalism which began to define the sky-lines of Chicago and New York at the turn of the century. The Chrysler Building, the Empire State Building, the Chanin Building, Rockefeller Center and Radio City Music Hall are supreme examples of the Art Deco style in urban America, although nearly every major town or city once boasted at least one Art Deco structure – post office, cinema, department store, or office building.

The Chrysler Building, at 42nd Street and Lexington Avenue, was designed in 1927 by William Van Alen for a real-estate developer, William H. Reynolds, who later sold the lease and plans to Walter P. Chrysler, the automobile magnate. The highly ornamented, 1046ft (319m) structure was completed in 1930, its soaring tower dramatically sheathed in shiny, nickel-chromed steel, in a design of overlapping arcs, punctuated by triangular windows. Just below this gleaming icing, at the 59th floor, an octet of stylized steel eagles play the roles of modernist gargoyles; considerably lower, at the 31st storey, exterior brickwork forms patterns of streamlined automobiles. The interior was deemed an unbalanced hodge-podge by many critics, but its individual elements – onyx lighting fixtures, handsome bronze mail slots incorporating a majestic eagle in their design, elevators with stylized flowers veneered in several types of wood, ceiling painting by Edward Turnbull – are all well-thought-out and exquisitely realized masterpieces in themselves.

**D**iagonally across from the Chrysler Building stands the 54-storey Chanin Building, which was erected in 1928 in a mere 205 days for the real-estate developer and architect Irwin Chanin. Although its boxy, stepped shape (designed by the firm of Sloan and Robertson) was neither especially remarkable nor innovative, its decoration, inside and out, was, celebrating the theme "City of Opportunity". The lobby features bronze allegorical relief-panels and radiator grilles, designed by René Chambellan and Jacques Delamarre, all rich with stylized figures and skyscrapers and embellished with a blaze of ziggurats, spirals, lightning bolts and starbursts. Piles of coins appropriately adorn the ornamental-ironwork entranceway to the top-floor executive suite.

The Empire State Building, on Fifth Avenue between 33rd and 34th streets, was completed in 1931 in a comparatively spare and modest style. Almost devoid of ornamentation, it is sheer height (1250ft, 412m), and the skilful massing of its 102 storeys that give it its rightful claim to fame. Even today, although it has been superseded by the World Trade Center (1350ft, 442m), it dominates midtown Manhattan, its massive stepped-pyramid body visible from miles away.

The Rockefeller Center complex, including Radio City Music Hall, was designed by Raymond Hood, who was responsible also for the Chicago Tribune Tower, as well as for New York's American Radiator, Daily News and McGraw-Hill Buildings. The three-block-long complex provided numerous Art Deco sculptors, designers, painters and other artists and artisans with glorious empty space to fill with bas-reliefs, figures, metalwork and wall and floor coverings. Radio City Music Hall, whose decoration was overseen and in large part undertaken by Donald Deskey, constitutes one gigantic tribute to Art Deco, with a wealth of metal-dominated modernist furniture and lighting fixtures, exotic-wood panelling, geometric ironwork, lavish painted murals, lively wallpaper and panels of carpeting. It is unabashedly opulent and exuberant.

Elsewhere in New York, skyscrapers, residential buildings and smaller office buildings bore decidedly *moderne* elements, including the Chanin Corporation's Century and Majestic apartment complexes on Central Park West (1930–31), the early New York Telephone Company building, now known as the Barclay-Vesey (1923), the Western Union Building on West Broadway (1928–30) and Ely Jacques Kahn's Film Center, 111 John Street, 120 Wall Street, Lefcourt Clothing Center and Squibb Building, all of which are marked by entranceways, lobbies, elevator doors and post boxes with geometric elements.

Art Deco shapes and ornamentation characterized not only buildings throughout the United States in the 1930s and 1940s, but also such vast engineering projects as the Hoover Dam, the towers of the Bay Bridge in San Francisco and the entrances to the

*Parisian architecture of the 1920s was generally traditional and restrained, not at all resembling the bold, often startling confections at the 1925 Paris Exposition. The Champs-Elysées building, above, is conservative yet modern, with its two-toned façade, moderne ironwork and clean lines.*

*The fantastic 1920s Los Angeles house, left, is by John Lloyd Wright (Frank's son). Looming over the front doorway is an amazing gaping jaw of stone, which encloses a window with a turquoise frame. The whole structure seems to be crawling out of the lush earth around it.*

Lincoln Tunnel, which connects New York to New Jersey.

Cinemas, too, were designed in the Art Deco style in the United States, and in Britain, where a clutch of Odeons still stand, paying tribute to the once-young art of movie-making with their geometric lighting fixtures, stylized murals and curtain designs, and other *moderne* elements. California movie theatres are, appropriately enough, the largest and most lavish examples of Art Deco cinemas, for example, Catalina Island's Avalon Theater, with its proscenium fire curtain depicting an angular Hermes symbolizing "The Flight of the Fancy Westward"; Los Angeles's Wiltern Theater, with its lavish star-studded ceiling and wildly over-decorated interior; the Pantages Theater, also in Los Angeles, rife with myriad floral, figural and geometric elements, mostly highlighted with gold leafing, and Oakland's Paramount Theater, designed by Timothy L. Pflueger, sheathed all over with ornamental ironwork and sculpted plaster in the "zigzag moderne" style, as some termed it. Indeed, the influences on cinema architecture were probably the most far-flung, eclectic and eccentric of all: Moorish, Egyptian, Aztec, American Indian, high-style French, mile-high New York and of course Hollywood itself.

In London, numerous other significant Art Deco buildings still exist, including the Savoy Theatre (1920), distinguished by its Egyptian-revival statues and urns; the Strand Palace Hotel (1930), literally dazzling with its angled illuminated glass panelling, and the Hoover Factory (1932) at Perivale, a curved, streamlined white sprawl, dotted with colourful Egypto-Aztec motifs.

The swansong of Art Deco architecture was spelled out, perhaps, with the 1939–40 World's Fair in New York, called "The World of Tomorrow" and dominated by its symbol, a massive geometric spear and globe, the Trylon and Perisphere. But in any case, by the end of the 1930s, Art Deco was already on the wane, its liveliness and decoration soon to give way to a pared-down, purely functional style which had been presaged in the designs decades earlier of Le Corbusier and the Bauhaus school, and in the straight, boxy structures of the American Modernists.

*The circle of the Liverpool Forum (now a Cannon cinema), left, is dominated by a peach-coloured relief panel of a hybrid landscape with two Manhattan-style skyscrapers flanking a curving river. The fluted pilasters (rectangular columns) around the panel are also architectonic.*

*The glittering façades of roadside diners beckoned to motorists all across the United States in the 1930s. The inside of the stainless-steel-sheathed Philadelphia diner, above, is doubtless brimming with shiny metal, Formica, booth-side jukeboxes and good home-cooked food.*

# FIGURAL MOTIFS

The massive leaping female, below, adorns the top of Leicester Square's Warner cinema, London. Actually, the figure is in triple-relief, with two silhouettes rippling out from behind the stone-carved nude.

The gaping-jawed stone head, right, is from Milan's Central Station. The 1931 building is by Eugenio Montuori and has been likened to a "monumental heap" that looks like a

"melting iceberg". The grotesque head, with its rectilinear headdress, is none the less an arresting example of Art Deco sculpture in Italy.

The Rex cinema in East Finchley, London, is an appropriate venue for the glittering frieze, left, which includes various symbols and instruments of Greek drama and entertainment within its borders – t mask, dagger and pipes among ther Other classical motifs – column, stylized wing – can be seen.

The BBC Building in London, left, is somewhat subdued and elegant. The 1932 structure (G. Val Mayer, architect) boasts decorations by Eric Gill and Vernon Hill. When it was built, the "New Tower of London", as it was called, was deemed too modern by some.

Sculptor Lee Lawrie collaborated with English-born ceramicist Leon V. Solon on the triptych, left, surmounting the entrance of 30 Rockefeller Plaza, part of the massive Rockefeller Center complex in Manhattan. In the middle is the figure Wisdom, who is flanked by Sound and Light. Solon's expertise was used in polychroming the reliefs. The subtly decorated cast-glass wall below the figures, comprising blocks of glass bonded by Vinylite (a type of polyvinyl chloride, or PVC) and reinforced by steel rods, was made by Steuben Glass.

Nearly every city in the US seems to possess at least one civic structure with Art Deco overtones. On the left is a detail of the Main Post Office in Kansas City (James A. Wetmore, architect), 1933–35. A stylized American eagle is carved in bas-relief on the corner; at the top is a neo-classical frieze with voluted components.

The carved-linoleum jungle mural, below, adorns the women's lounge of Union Terminal in Cincinnati. Jean Bourdelle was its designer in c.1931. The African motifs are in the high-style Parisian mode, similar to some of the subjects which appear on Jean Dunand's lacquered screens.

...lan's Central Station, above, was ...ilt in 1931 (Eugenio Montuori, ...chitect). Though following a long ...dition of monumental architecture, ... massive stone pile does possess ...oderne design elements, including ...ometric motifs and stylized equine, ...nine and human figures.

...colourful fire-curtain, left, ...minates the stage of the 1929 ...ckwick Theatre in Park Ridge, ...nois (R. Harold Zook and M. ...ughey, architects). Stylized leaves ...d berries, a flock of tropical birds ...d a smattering of geometric motifs ...mprise the curtain, over which ...ree tiers of earthy-toned zigzags ...d other vaguely Mayan decorative ...ments dazzle.

# METAL

The directory in the foyer of New York's Film Centre below (Ely Jacques Kahn, architect) is bold and rectilinear, and punctuated by bright red letters and dots.

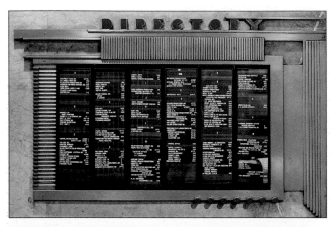

The door of the Gulf Building in Houston, left, clearly takes its inspiration from high-style Parisian design, notably that of ironworker Edgar Brandt.

William Van Alen's glittering Chrysler Building, above, is still a jewel on Manhattan's skyline. It is crowned by a 27-ton nickel-chromed steel spire, comprising five gradating haloes studded with triangular windows. The 1930 skyscraper also boasts eagle gargoyles at the 59th-storey setback and winged radiator caps on the 31st floor.

The grandiose Reception Hall of London's Daily Express building, below, on Fleet Street, is decorated with sheets of shiny white and yellow metal. The 1931 entrance hall, designed by Robert Atkinson, was admired by John Betjeman for its "wonderful rippling confections of metal".

The chief architect of New York's McGraw-Hill Building (now Group Health Insurance), above left, was Raymond Hood, collaborating with Frederick Godley and Jacques Fouilhoux. The 1931 granite-clad tower – which Vincent Scully has called "proto-jukebox modern" – is embellished at street level with polished metal, as seen left, and on its upper 34 storeys with green terracotta tiling.

Monel metal (a nickel-copper alloy) sheathes a lift interior, right, at Unilever House, London, built in the 1930s (J. Lomax Simpson, architect). The two panels on the right depict modern modes of transport.

The opulent decoration of New York's Chanin Building, on 42nd Street and Lexington Avenue, was not confined to the façade and lobby. Below is the tiled Executive Suite bathroom, which was reserved for Irwin S. Chanin. Its decoration, like that of the entire building, was supervised by Jacques Delamarre, who was the department head of the massive Chanin Construction Company.

Cream, gold and green tiles domina[te] the room (note especially the row of avian tiles near the ceiling, which hides a ventilating duct), but the outstanding features are the sunbur[st] pattern over the engraved-glass shower doors, and the shower and basin taps (see left) which were gol[d] plated. The building's architects wer[e] Sloan & Robertson; it dates from 1929.

The bronze radiator grille, above, is in the foyer of New York's Chanin Building. The architectonic grille and a figurative plaque above it were jointly termed Endurance. René Chambellan designed both in collaboration with Jacques Delamarre.

The handsome lift door, right, is from New York's Chrysler Building. Veneered in the Tyler Company's METYL-WOOD is a lotus design, the beauty of which suffers from its clashing marble surround.

# METAL

Sparkling like a latter-day Versailles, the Hall of Mirrors, right, is in the Starrett Netherland Plaza Hotel, Carew Tower, Cincinnati (Walter W. Ahlschlager, architect). The recently restored hotel dates from 1931, and is one of several outstanding examples of Art Deco architecture in the Ohio city. The ornamental balustrade's floral and neo-classical devices borrow from high-style Parisian design, namely that of Edgar Brandt, while the armature of the hanging lamps is reminiscent of work of the Wiener WerkstÑtte's Dagobert Peche. Most of the hotel's innovative lighting devices were provided by E. F. Caldwell & Co. The Starrett Netherland's Continental Room and Palm Court are equally lavish.

The pair of handsome lift doors, right, are covered in monel metal, a nickel-copper alloy (named after A. Monell, president of the American firm which introduced the material). The doors adorn the lobby of the First National City Trust Co, once the City Bank Farmers Trust Co, in the Wall Street area of Manhattan.

One of the highlights of London's plush Park Lane Hotel, opened in 1927, is the Art Deco ballroom, left. Palmette, shell and swag motifs embellish the cream-coloured room, which is dominated by an overdoor painted-plaster relief of Bellerophon and his glittering steed Pegasus.

# MOTIFS

The glittering embellishments on the upper portion of the Art Deco office building in London, below, are part-Camelot, part-Luxor – and a jaunty feather-in-the-cap on the starkly square lines of the structure itself. The Eastern-Columbia Building in Los Angeles, right (Claud Beelman, architect), is sheathed in glazed aquamarine and gold terracotta tiles, with recessed copper spandrels. The stepped structure was built in the 1930s as a retail centre.

Seen in two photographs, above, is the Hoover factory (Wallis, Gilbert & Partners, architects), situated in Perivale, outside London. The semi-streamlined 1930s complex features vivid colours, geometric details and sunburst designs – although it essentially subscribes to Le Corbusier's maxim that buildings "should be white by law". Many other modern factories from the Art Deco era have since been demolished; luckily the Hoover building has not.

The Firestone factory in London, right, was sadly razed in 1982. Its white surface was enhanced by neo-Egyptian, classical and Moorish elements, and its exterior metalwork was in the modern style – for example, the two lamps at the entranceway.

ght, the façade of the Odeon in the
ssex Road, London, a detail of which
atures Egyptian-Revival columns
d stylized lotuses. The former
nema is now a bingo hall.

e imposing front of the
iladelphia Music School of c.1929,
low, includes a stepped upper
ction and terracotta decoration in
ometric configurations. The long
ng-like design at the bottom was
ost likely repeated in the horizontal
tween-window sections above it.

The ebullient decoration on the façade
of the present-day Kansas City retail
store, left, dates to c.1929
(McKecknie & Trask, architects). The
salient feature is the glazed terracotta
tiling in a busy floral, geometric and
neo-classical pattern. Note the three
lighting fixtures and the clever rayed
design in coloured clay below them.

Although fast disappearing from
American byways, petrol stations, like
the Gulf one below in Bedford,
Pennsylvania, were once a delightful
commonplace. The 1930s structure
resembles an Egyptian temple, and
the geometric and neo-classical motifs
on its terracotta tiles are typical of
much commercial architecture of
the time.

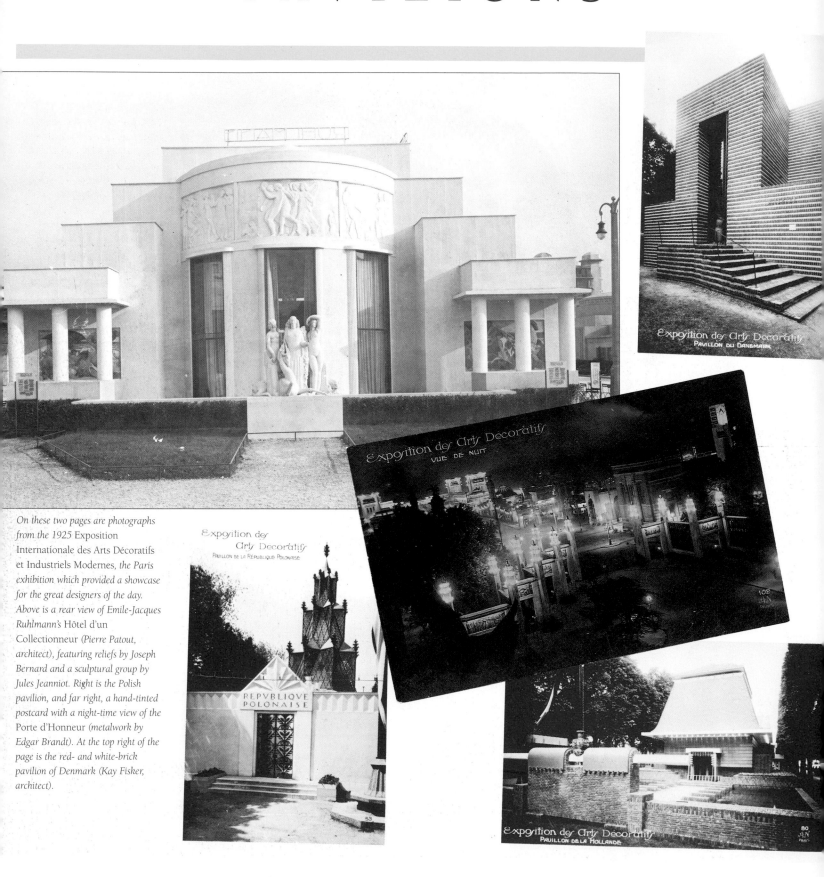

On these two pages are photographs from the 1925 Exposition Internationale des Arts Décoratifs et Industriels Modernes, *the Paris exhibition which provided a showcase for the great designers of the day. Above is a rear view of Emile-Jacques Ruhlmann's Hôtel d'un Collectionneur (Pierre Patout, architect), featuring reliefs by Joseph Bernard and a sculptural group by Jules Jeanniot. Right is the Polish pavilion, and far right, a hand-tinted postcard with a night-time view of the Porte d'Honneur (metalwork by Edgar Brandt). At the top right of the page is the red- and white-brick pavilion of Denmark (Kay Fisker, architect).*

Exposition des Arts Décoratifs
PAVILLON DU DANEMARK

Exposition des Arts Décoratifs
VUE DE NUIT

Exposition des
Arts Décoratifs
PAVILLON DE LA RÉPUBLIQUE POLONAISE

REPVBLIQVE POLONAISE

Exposition des Arts Décoratifs
PAVILLON DE LA HOLLANDE

Exposition des
Arts Decoratifs
PAVILLON DE L'AFRIQUE OCCIDENTALE

Exposition des
Arts Decoratifs

The Pavillon du Tourisme of Robert
Mallet-Stevens, seen in the gouache,
left, was a natural beacon at the Fair.
The less imposing tower, below, was
part of the Austrian pavilion,
conceived by Josef Hoffmann, whose
proto-moderne creations of c.1900
were harbingers of Art Deco design.

Exposition d
Arts Decora

PAVILLON DE L'AUTRICHE

PAVILLON TCHÉCO-SLOVAQUE

mong the various pavilions at the
025 Exposition were those of
olland, left (J. F. Stael, architect),
zechoslovakia, above (Josef Gočár,
chitect), and top, with a cactus-like
me, West Africa. Right is Le
orbusier's pavilion, L'Esprit
ouveau, a handsome white box
ilt around a tree; his "house"
used a scandal, even though it was
true signal of the Machine Age.

Match de Boxe (Boxing Match), *fashion-plate from Art, Goût, Beauté, France, May 1923*

# CHAPTER • SEVEN

# FASHION, JEWELLERY, AND ACCESSORIES

Fashion played an important role in Art Deco design, not only in terms of its direct influence on other mediums – the Ballets Russes costumes, for instance, made waves – but also because many of its leading lights, Paul Poiret, Jacques Doucet and Jeanne Lanvin among them, were extraordinary collectors and tastemakers who helped enormously to promote Le Style 25.

Fashion illustration was significant as well; not only did the drawings of Paul Iribe, Georges Lepape, George Barbier and Erté help in themselves to spread the new couture, but their styles and use of vivid colours had a strong influence on many other artists in France and elsewhere.

Fashion accessories – handbags, powder compacts, fans, cigarette cases – were designed in abundance in the 1920s and 1930s, often with bold geometric and floral motifs that were every bit as masterful as those decorating furniture, ceramics and textiles. Jewellery, too, reflected the spirit of modernism, whether made of precious stones and metals – by Cartier, Tiffany or Van Cleef & Arpels – or of lesser materials such as glass, plastic, paste and base metal, sometimes by anonymous designers, sometimes by those as renowned as René Lalique.

In Parisian fashion design, as in other mediums, the influence of the Ballets Russes was paramount. Sergei Diaghilev's company had invaded the French capital in 1909, and its oriental splendour – in costumes, scenery and the dance itself – transformed the course of Gallic design. Almost immediately, Léon Bakst's exotic creations, his ornamental, brightly hued and sumptuous fabrics, began to be reflected in French couture. At the same time the impact of Paul Poiret (1879–1944) was being felt. Having started his career working for both Worth and Doucet, he had already begun to make his name by 1906, with his fluid dress designs distinguished by their smooth, corset-less line. In 1908, Paul Iribe had produced a set of vividly coloured pochoirs (stencilled ink drawings) illustrating his new fashions, Les Robes de Paul Poiret. His creations, coupled with those of the Ballets Russes, heralded a new era, not only in design but in illustration as well. Preceding most of Art Deco by at least a decade, they were very much in the forefront of the style.

Poiret himself advanced the entire style, with the workshop he founded in 1912, the Atelier Martine, where he employed young working-class girls whose charming drawings and designs were the basis of rugs, fabrics, wallpapers, furniture and lamps which he marketed through his Maison Martine.

Besides the straight, sleek, sometimes empire-waisted dresses which liberated the Art Deco woman from painful corsets and bulky petticoats, she could be seen wearing exotic turbans, often bejewelled or plumed, small cloche hats and bandeaux perched above the eyebrows. By the end of the First World War, hems were almost universally short, but still below the knee, and waists began to be dropped. Busts became de-emphasized, and backless dresses – declarations of freedom – abounded for evening. Colours were bright, sometimes outrageously so, and patterns were bold, usually floral. Hairstyles also reflected women's post-war independence, becoming short and cropped or "bobbed".

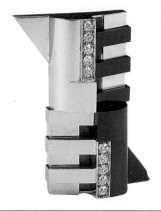

*The 1928 brooch, right, is by Gérard Sandoz, the Paris jeweller. Of gold, onyx, enamel and diamonds, the brooch has a strong geometric form characteristic of Sandoz's work, most of which he produced in a period of 10 years; he later explored painting and film.*

*The exotic evening coat, below, was designed by Paul Poiret, the influential Art Deco couturier. From La Gazette du Bon Ton (1920), the fashion-plate was created by George Lepape. The tassels, cap and colours are characteristic of Poiret.*

ANTINÉA

Manteau du soir, de Paul Poiret

...eral American jewellers produced ...cious Art Deco pieces, although ...angely, most of their designers ...mained anonymous. The c.1928 ...awing, right, is of a diamond and ...pphire necklace by Oscar Heyman ...d Bros.

...1925 Charles Massé designed the ...tinum, coral, onyx and diamond ...ooch, below, for Boucheron. ...mbining semi-precious stones with ...ecious metal and gems became a ...mmonplace in Art Deco Paris. ...ral and onyx were popular as a ...ndsome complement to silvery ...tinum.

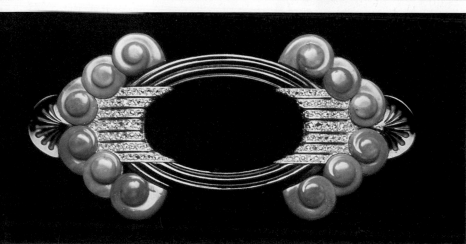

Coco Chanel revolutionized haute couture with her chic daytime designs, including the classic short and tailored two-piece suit. Besides Poiret and Chanel, the top designers included Elsa Schiaparelli (who, among her classic costumes, wittily designed a hat topped by a shoe, and a gown shaped like a lobster), Jean Patou, Madeleine Vionnet (who invented the bias cut), Christian Berard, Mainbocher, Paquin, Lucien Lelong, Jacques Doucet and Jeanne Lanvin.

Sonia Delaunay's Paris designs were influenced by the geometric elements of fine art, such as her brightly checked or zigzagged coats, dresses and hats (she even had a car's body decorated with a similar geometric motif!). Delaunay's creations were quite similar to the avant-garde designs by the Russians Stepanova and Popova, with their practical lines and severe cuts, and quite removed from the heavily ornamented exotic costumes of Poiret.

Then as now, styles changed from season to season, of course, with hemlines constantly fluctuating, waistlines appearing and disappearing, skirts growing slimmer or fuller. None the less, the great early Paris couturiers dramatically brought fashion to the fore, making it as influential as any other design medium, a circumstance that has remained constant in the six or seven decades since they first made their mark.

Jewellery and accessories in the Art Deco period were as varied and colourful as the fashions themselves. Great French goldsmiths fashioned miniature works of art in platinum, gold, diamonds, emeralds and other precious gems – some starkly geometric, others with Egyptian or oriental overtones, still others wildly florid and encrusted with stones of many colours. Such hardstones as onyx, turquoise, jade and lapis lazuli were also used, and enamelling was widely applied.

Unlike Art Nouveau jewellery, which often involved realistic floral, figural or faunal motifs, Art Deco tended to be simpler; it was usually either geometric or abstract, and even when it featured flowers or other realistic elements, was quite subtle and underplayed. The fashions of the day – cloche hats, short hair, short hemlines, short sleeves – demanded complementary jewellery forms and types. Brooches were worn on hat brims, on shoulders, on hips, on belts; long strands of beads, or sautoirs, hung from the neck; bracelets and bangles of all kinds adorned the arm, and dangling earrings and small ear clips appeared in myriad handsome guises. In addition, both fancy wrist and pendant watches appeared. Mauboussin, Lacloche Frères, Fouquet, Boucheron, Cartier, Chaumet and Van Cleef & Arpels were some of the major jewellers, whose output included not only standard jewellery items, but also powder compacts and cigarette cases. These became *de rigueur* in the 1920s for the bold woman of fashion, who could now both smoke and powder her nose in public. Inexpensive versions of all these items were fashioned of paste, plastic and base metal. The application of coloured enamel to the metal pieces often made them, despite being cheap and mass-produced, every bit as handsome as the more expensive models.

Several renowned goldsmiths created lovely, often one-of-a-kind jewels for their exclusive clientele. Georges Fouquet, who had designed outstanding Art Nouveau jewels, adapted quite easily to the more spare, but no less spectacular, designs of the Art Deco period. His son Jean was even bolder and more original, his geometric creations often resembling Cubist sculptures.

Jean Dunand, the famous lacquerworker (see the section on furniture), also designed brooches, earrings and bracelets, usually of hammered silver and embellished with geometric designs in black, red and gold lacquer, that echoed the polygonal shapes of the pieces themselves. He produced a striking pair of earrings with dangling black enamel grids which were reminiscent of the "gitterwerk" of turn-of-the-century Vienna.

Gérard Sandoz, who also designed modernist silver tea sets (se the section on metalwork), created jewels very much in th Machine Age vein, with smooth shiny or matt metal "part featuring materials like onyx and coral and punctuated by a sing aquamarine "stud" or a line of diamonds. This work spanned on about a decade, unfortunately; he later turned to film-making ar painting.

Raymond Templier, whose grandfather founded the fami jewellery firm in 1849, fashioned outstanding jewels, son combining several metals and stones in unusually handsom settings. A bracelet containing a brooch in the Virginia Museum Fine Art's collection in Richmond, Va, is an outstanding example his intricate designs: the wide silver band centres on a removab brooch of platinum, white gold and diamonds which is itse rectilinear but which features a large round diamond.

The Cartier firm produced more traditional and less geometr jewels, Louis Cartier often being influenced by the arts of Egyp the Islamic world and the Orient, as well as by the craftsmansh of the legendary Peter Carl Fabergé, goldsmith of the Russian roy family. Compared with the bold, stark designs of Templier, Sand et al, Cartier's jewels were extremely decorative, even pictorial; created vanity cases adorned with Chinese landscapes in mothe of-pearl, coloured enamels and rubies, and diamond brooches the form of overflowing flower baskets. His timepieces we especially fabulous – such rich confections as a mantel clock wi a carved-jade face, a frame of gold, black enamel and coral ar gold hands shaped like a dragon and spear. He also devis "mystery clocks" which seemed to run without any works; the were in fact hidden by means of an ingenious optical device.

René Lalique, the undisputed *maître verrier* (see the section glass), designed spectacular glass jewellery, including round ar oval medallions moulded with female figures, insects and flowe some in bright hues, others in subtly stained frosted glass. He al created rings, expanding bracelets, necklaces of small glass bead and brooches and buckles backed by foil and metal.

American jewellery in the Art Deco period was most designed in the French style by fine firms such as Tiffar Udall & Ballou, Spaulding-Gorham and C. D. Peacoc Bracelets, brooches and pendants were sometimes stark geometric, but far more often were either simple flor arrangements or dazzling masses of coloured gems and diamond

Elsewhere, the style was neither widespread nor much imitate although occasional pieces were produced in Italy, Germany ar Britain during the late 1920s. Switzerland's watchmakers, who designers were often French, created cases with subtle geometr motifs, and Georg Jensen, the Danish silversmith, fashione necklaces, brooches and buckles in both gold and silver, usually open-work with stylized animals and flowers.

The Art Deco period also spawned thousands of chea anonymous designs, many of which are highly sought after collectors today. These included bracelets, brooches, barettes ar clips – for ears, shoes, lapels – in coloured Bakelite, celluloid ar

*The white-metal, diamanté and carved-stone belt buckle, below, was made in Czechoslovakia, as was so much of the mass-produced jewellery in the 1920s and 30s, and particularly pieces made of glass. The stylized berry-and-leaf design in black is especially lovely.*

*The wide bracelet, right, is made of platinum, silver, gold, diamonds and onyx. It was created c.1925–30 by Raymond Templier, whose works often bore strong geometric shapes. The centre section can be removed from the silver band and displayed as a brooch.*

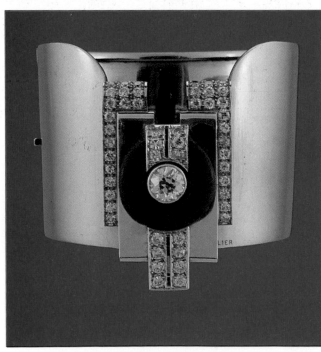

...her synthetics, often in geometric shapes or carved as stylized ...wers. Czechoslovakia, long a producer of glass beads, made ...expensive necklaces, pins and other bits of jewellery which were ...metimes quite striking, with strong angles and colours.

Mass-produced compacts and vanity cases also proliferated, especially in France and the United States. These were sometimes marked with the cosmetics firm's ...me – Richard Hudnut, Coty, Helena Rubinstein – but more often ...graved with such evocative words as Volupté or Zanadu. One ...ty compact was covered all over with a René Lalique design of ...lized powder puffs, in black, orange, white and gold; the same ...sign appeared on a cardboard powder box and is in production ...ain today. Firms manufacturing industrial metal, such as Elgin ...merican in Illinois, diversified to produce compacts and vanity ...ses which were often superbly engineered in enamelled chrome ...other white metal and which sold for a dollar or less. Many of ...e cheaper varieties sported figural or faunal designs – stylishly ...ad ladies, graceful deer or greyhounds, playful Scotties. ...namelled cigarette cases for both men and women were covered ...th rich geometric, sunburst or zigzag patterns, or adorned with ...stone stud or two.

Fans ranged from simple contemporary designs in paper (often ...th an advertisement on the reverse side) to delicate silk and satin ...tasies on carved wooden frames. The mother-of-pearl fans ...eated by Frenchman Georges Bastard were perhaps the most ...vish accessories of the time, their delicate ribs patterned with ...lized flowers, triangles or other geometric shapes. Bastard also ...signed boxes, bowls, lanterns and a wide range of jewels – ...ngles, hatpins, haircombs – in mother-of-pearl, ivory, jade, ...rtoiseshell, horn, rock crystal and coral.

Handbags were usually quite small, either "clutch" style or with ...ndles. They were sometimes covered with elaborate beading that ...as suspended from jewel-encrusted silver frames, or perhaps ...ade of lizard, snakeskin or sharkskin (shagreen). In the United ...ates, steel mesh bags appeared, their metal frames frequently ...corated with geometric designs in colourful enamels or studded ...th cut-steel "jewels" known as marcasites (these were also ...pular diamond substitutes in cheap jewellery). Brocade, ...nbroidered and tapestry bags were plentiful as well, adorned ...ther with jazzy geometric designs or colourful floral patterns. By ...e late 1930s, plastic was emerging as a stylish material, and ...lky handbags, often round or rectangular, began to be carried, ...metimes even by women of taste.

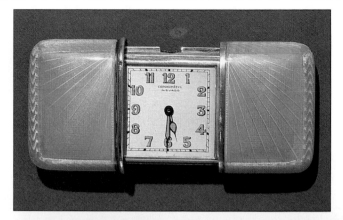

*Labelled Chronomètre on its face, the Movado silver pocket watch, left, has a lovely enamelled case with an apt sunburst design. The square face, with its traditional numerals painted yellow, is revealed by sliding the two enamelled sides apart.*

*The assortment of ladies' beaded bags, above, from the 1920s and 30s, presents an array of floral and geometric designs. The crocheted purse on the lower left is embellished with metallic beading, and the amber and gold example on the lower right has two paste-studded plastic bangles serving as handles.*

# DRESS

*The flowing Crêpe de Chine dresses the women wear in the fashion-plate below, from the magazine Art, Goût, Beauté, sport the new dropped waist of the 1920s.*

*Le Messager (The Messenger) right, by Edouard Halouze, features a dreamy-eyed woman in a low-cut, bejewelled gown. The lush flowerscape background is pure Art Deco.*

*The 1919 stencil, right, is by George Barbier, one of Paris' best-known illustrators. It is from the 1919 Guirlande des Mois, one of five silk-bound almanacs he designed. The books contained 12 stencils which were reproduced by a delicate stencilling process. The faintly suggestive pose of the two women, who question a cockatoo, was not unusual for liberated, post-war Paris.*

A PALM BEACH

TAILLEUR, DE WORTH

## PAUL POIRET

Parisian fashion designer Paul Poiret (1879–1944) was the beacon of *haute couture's* leading lights in the Art Deco era. He began his career working for the houses of Jacques Doucet and Worth, and by 1906 he was making a name for himself – chiefly due to his smooth-flowing, corsetless fashions, which in effect liberated twentieth-century woman from the past. The bright colours and exotic, oriental aspects of his fashions derived from his love of Indian and Persian art and his admiration of the Ballets Russes.

But Poiret was not only a dress designer. He was also a patron of the arts and true arbiter of Art Deco taste, supporting young artists and collecting their works, creating perfumes, publishing books, holding fancy costume balls and in 1912 establishing a design studio and workshop, the Atelier Martine (named after his daughter), which produced upholstery and curtain fabrics, carpets, furniture, even dolls. Whole interior-design schemes were a product of Poiret and his atelier, not only for his own residences but also for those of others.

*George Barbier's rather sedate fashion-plate at left, from La Gazette du Bon Ton (1921), spotlights a handsome resort-wear suit by Worth. The hemline is quite short, especially compared to the high neck of the collar.*

The fashion-plate at left appeared in Art, Goût, Beauté (1921). The slim line of the dress, its high neck and the elaborate plumed hat were common features of 1920s haute couture. The puffy, tasselled pillows, too, are very much of the Art Deco period.

The Barbier stencil below, from La Gazette du Bon Ton, shows a high-stepping dancer in a low-waisted dress, the revealing top aglow with flowers. The close-fitting cap was a typical head-covering of the day. The setting is the 1925 Paris Exposition.

## LA DANSEUSE AUX JETS D'EAU
ROBE DE DANSE, DE WORTH

LA DOUCE NUIT

L'HEURE DU THÉ

LES EMBARRAS DE PARIS
Manteau d'après-midi, de Doeuillet

The three stylish fashion-plates at left feature, from left to right, fashions by Worth, Lanvin and Doeuillet. They depict, respectively, a charming evening interlude, stepping into a tea-time rendezvous, and a Paris traffic jam. A. E. Marty painted the left and right images, Benito the centre one. All are from 1920 issues of La Gazette du Bon Ton.

French fashion illustration of the Art Deco period influenced other European and American artists. At top, an advertisment from a European magazine, featuring an ermine-swaddled 1920s woman. Her turban was first made popular by couturier Paul Poiret, her Cupid's-bow lips and heavily shadowed eyes by Hollywood actresses.

The holiday greeting card on the right, c.1925, is signed "Renbal". The fluffy white collar, cuffs and lining of the woman's scarlet coat are rather exaggerated, and the shocking-pink hue of her top hat, gloves and flowing ribbons at odds with the rest of her outfit. Yet the off-centre image works well in its ephemeral, non-fashion-plate context, especially against the lush gold ground.

Art - Goût - Beauté

The French fashion-plate, left, from the January 1923 issue of Art, Goût, Beauté features a woman wearing a stunning black wool ensemble. Except for the jet black of the costume, the palette of the plate is pastel, and quite unwintry. The subject's two companions help give the scene a narrative context.

# GEOMETRIC

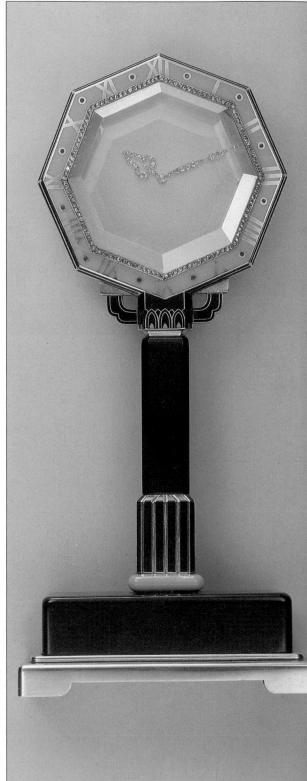

Geometric designs adorned jewellery
and fashion accessories both precious
and costume. The three tiny
timepieces, above, with Swiss-made
works and elaborate frames, could be
worn as brooches or pendants.
Though of rhinestones and paste,
their forms mimic those of expensive
jewellers' works.

The Cartier firm produced so-called
"mystery clocks", including the one
from 1921, right, for a wealthy
clientele. The works of these stunning
jewels were cleverly hidden by means
of an optical device. This clock is
vaguely Egyptian in its colours, gold-
leaf design and basic stepped form.

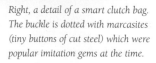

The Greek-key design on the frame of
the handsome handbag, above, fits
nicely into the Art Deco repertory,
being both classical and geometric.
The metal and cloth bag is probably
French.

Right, a detail of a smart clutch bag.
The buckle is dotted with marcasites
(tiny buttons of cut steel) which were
popular imitation gems at the time.

The stunning pendant at right is by
[La]cloche Frères, among Paris'
[pr]emier jewellers. Fashioned from
[pl]atinum, diamonds, onyx and pearl,
[it]s form is simple and geometric.

[T]he stepped-pyramid form of the
[en]amelled metal powder compact,
[be]low, is intentionally architectonic:
[it] is a 1930s souvenir from the
[Em]pire State Building, whose form is
[sk]etchily rendered on the piece in
[sh]ades of green.

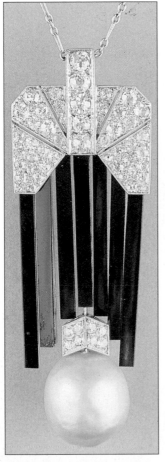

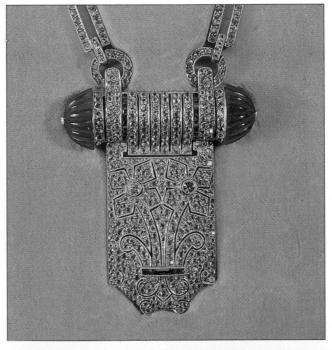

The French necklace on the left dates
from the mid-1920s, and is made of
silver, paste and jade. Its squared-off
design is quite geometric, even down
to the two stylized flowers which are
outlined on the pendant. The chain is
especially handsome, alternating
nicely articulated rectangular and
circular forms of diamanté-studded
silver.

The American powder compact, left,
is from the late 1930s. The base
yellow metal has been 'frosted' in
places to create a handsome
geometric motif.

The 1920s silver gilt table watch,
above, is by Meyrowitz, and sports
green- and black-enamelled wings at
its sides. Its square face is strongly
geometric, its gilt numerals rendered
in an Art Deco-style typography.

The sunray pattern on the face was
found on many 1920s pieces, but it
has its root in earlier goldsmiths'
work, such as that of the Russian
Peter Carl Fabergé.

# FIGURATIVE

As it became more and more acceptable for a woman to smoke in public in the post-war 1920s, so she needed lovely accessories. The famed Cartier firm created the stunning cigarette case right, in mother-of-pearl, coral and diamonds. The elaborate oriental landscape depicted on the case is as beautiful as that on any Japanese screen. Note especially the tiny turtle with red shell.

Powder compacts both bejewelled and non-precious were produced in vast quantities in the 1920s and 1930s. The enamelled metal quartet, above, are of French and American origin (the open one reveals a patent number). In actuality, the impeccable tooling and engineering of these feminine accessories were often due to the skills of a talented male industrial designer. The figures on the four here present attractive silhouettes, notably the red and black example with its musicians and dancing couple.

The simple enamelled metal box, below, contains nail-care tools by the American cosmetics firm Cutex. The well-manicured hands of the almond-eyed lady are duly emphasized. The set would have been made in huge numbers and sold for very little at the likes of Woolworth's.

CUTEX FIVE MINUTE SET

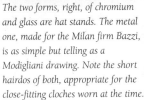

The enamelled silver cigarette case above is English and dates from 1931. The dancing couple portrayed on the lid wear loose oriental-style costumes, cut in jazzy Art Deco colours and patterns – no doubt more than a passing nod to both the Ballets Russes and French couturier Paul Poiret.

The two forms, right, of chromium and glass are hat stands. The metal one, made for the Milan firm Bazzi, is as simple but telling as a Modigliani drawing. Note the short hairdos of both, appropriate for the close-fitting cloches worn at the time.

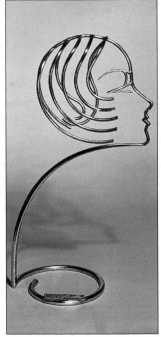
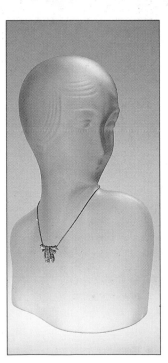

# PRECIOUS

## LOUIS CARTIER

Louis Cartier (1875–1942) was the third generation of his family to head the House of Cartier in Paris, which had been founded by his grandfather in 1847. The year marked a significant change in the output of the firm, brought about in part by Louis' fascination with the Ballets Russes and Islamic art. The colours and designs on Cartier's jewels became quite daring and innovative, as did the actual composition of the pieces, which now featured both precious and semiprecious gems in dramatic settings.

Bold geometric patterns appeared, but even more common to Cartier's repertory were figurative motifs inspired by the exotic worlds of India, Egypt, and the Middle and Far East. By 1920, Cartier's *oeuvre* included such luxury *objets* as vanity cases, jewel caskets, lighters and timepieces.

Cartier's "mystery clocks", introduced in 1913, contained an ingenious optical device which seemed to cause the hands to rotate on their hardstone faces without any visible works.

*Van Cleef & Arpels, one of France's most exclusive jewellers, created the two vanity cases on the right. The top one is primarily of lapis lazuli, including its centre panel of carved flowers dotted with diamonds. The overall motif is Egyptian-looking, with the two rock-crystal sunrays at the sides resembling a Pharaonic head-dress. The bottom case features a lovely Japanese landscape of inlaid gold, abalone and mother-of-pearl. Louis Arpels is credited with inventing the copyrighted minaudière, the ultimate lady's fashion accessory which housed compartments for powder, rouge, lipstick, comb, sometimes even a watch.*

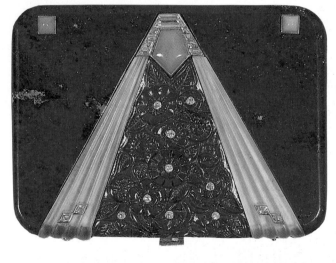

*The above three jewels, brooches at top and centre, ring below, were designed by Parisian Jean Fouquet, whose father, Georges, was also a jeweller. The combination of the semiprecious stones onyx and coral with diamonds and platinum is typical of the time.*

*Below are two stunning Art Deco pieces, a cigarette holder set with diamonds and distinguished by an amber mouthpiece, and a Cartier brooch comprising a stylized flower basket of lapis lazuli, enamel, diamonds and turquoise.*

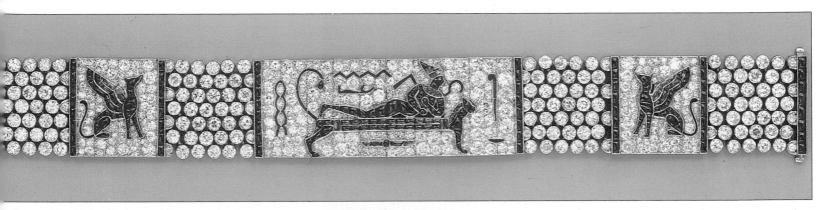

The diamond, ruby, emerald and sapphire bracelet, above, exemplifies the Egyptian-revival aspect of Art Deco, spurred on by the 1922 discovery of Tutankhamen's tomb. A regal figure reclines on an animal-shaped daybed; hieroglyph designs float overhead. The maker is Lacloche Frères.

The pair of drop-earrings, below, were fashioned by Boucheron of Paris. Of jade, onyx and diamonds, the long, dangling jewels would have been nicely shown off by a fashionably short haircut.

aris' Lacloche Frères created the unning bangle, above, a suitable omplement to the revealing new shions of the 1920s, which often red the arms, necks and legs, begging them to be covered with jewels. Of rock crystal, diamonds, rubies and coloured enamel, the armpiece features facing dolphins. The sea animals were a motif drawn from classical Greece and Rome. Interestingly, Lacloche took over Fabergé's London shop after the Russian Revolution.

The two bangles, below, are moulded of phenolic resin, a type of plastic which is easily coloured and was therefore popular for mass-production jewellery. These brightly hued bracelets are from the 1930s.

The attractive set on the right includes ear-clips, necklace and expandable bracelet of gilt-metal ar[d] casein, a type of plastic made from skim milk curdled with rennet. The bright red rectangles are arranged i[n] a dentate pattern, one found on ma[ny] Art Deco creations, from furniture t[o] ceramics.

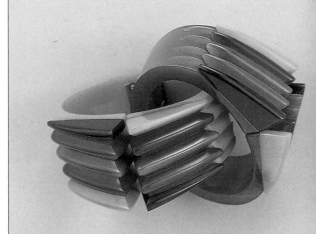

The boxes and brooch, above, were "carved" in plastic in the 1920s. Their creamy hue is reminiscent of ivory, and the boxes are vaguely oriental-looking. Plastics can be natural (from resins, as in Chinese lacquerwork, which came into widespread use in the 1800s) or synthetic; the bulk of Art Deco plastics – including Bakelite (named after its inventor, Leo Baekeland), celluloid and casein – fall into the man-made category. Plastics were used to produce fashion accessories ranging from vivid jewellery to rather cumbersome handbags. Even the glass-maker René Lalique once turned his skills to plastic, designing a square box in dark red celluloid with a still-life design.

**NEW YORK TO PARIS
MAY 21, 1927**

**KING OF THE AIR**

The charming aeroplane pin, left, st[ill] attached to its original paper backin[g] commemorates the historic transatlantic flight of Charles Lindbergh, the "King of the Air", in 1927. Such early souvenir items can be considered forerunners of today's pop-star and political badges. The plane's rather simple design is not at all like that of the streamlined commercial flying machines which took to the air in the 1930s.

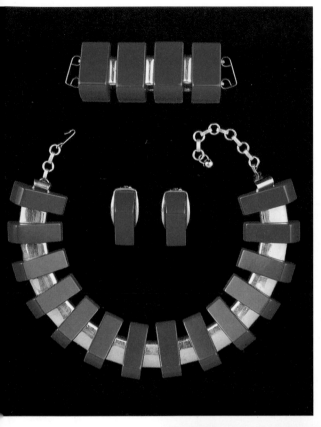

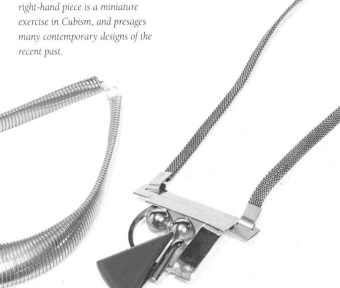

The chrome necklaces, below, are both strikingly set off by pieces of bright synthetic plastic. The chains are intricately fashioned, solid yet flexible and easily worn. The pendant on the right-hand piece is a miniature exercise in Cubism, and presages many contemporary designs of the recent past.

Elgin American, a firm located near Chicago, Illinois, was a successful producer of assorted women's and men's accessories of the 1930s. The compact and matching lipstick case, right, is handsomely presented as a boxed set, perfect for gift-giving. Compacts were popular presents in the Art Deco era, and many women received them, complete with monograms, from the man (or men) in their lives. Elgin watches are still produced today.

The striking geometric design on the rouge box, above, includes the cosmetics line's name, Princess Pat. A 1930s advertisement for the product promised to make customers "all fragrant and beautiful – all charming – all serenely perfect".

The Comet, *silvered bronze and marble, Maurice Guiraud Riviere, France, c.1925*

# CHAPTER • EIGHT
# PAINTING AND SCULPTURE

# PAINTING AND SCULPTURE

Painting and sculpture in the Art Deco period had tremendous variety; it could be decorative or avant-garde, sleekly streamlined or lushly ornamented, highly representational or markedly abstract. Not all works of art painted or carved in the 1920s and 1930s can, of course, be termed Art Deco, since the term is generally applied to design and not to fine art. Still, some artists' works, whether because of their use of colour and geometric motifs, their stylization, or, more frequently, their inclusion in contemporary interior decoration or architecture, are considered outstanding examples of the genre.

In painting, the premier exponent of the Art Deco style was probably Tamara de Lempicka (1898–1980), a Warsaw-born beauty who emigrated to Paris from Russia in the 1920s, and later to the United States. Between 1924 and 1939 she painted about 100 portraits and nudes; these were dramatically composed works, usually boldly coloured (but sometimes black and white), highly stylized and charged with energy, sensuality and sophistication. Partly angled Cubism, partly fashion illustration, they were positive expressions of the Art Deco style.

In sharp contrast to her handsome, somewhat aggressive works were the ethereal paintings of Marie Laurençin, which are often characterized as highly feminine because of their pastel hues, female subjects and innate "prettiness". They were strong, distinctive images nonetheless, and they appeared prominently in contemporary interiors, including those of her brother-in-law André Groult. She also designed carpets and created stage-sets and costumes for the Ballets Russes production of Francis Poulenc's *Les Biches*.

Female figures dominated Art Deco canvases, and nowhere more boldly than in the paintings of Bordeaux-trained Raphael Delorme, whose bulky, muscular nudes were often situated in bizarre architectural settings, wearing only incongruous head-dress or surrounded by fully dressed maidservants. Indeed, an entire group of Bordeaux artists emerged in the Art Deco period, including not only Delorme but also Jean Dupas, Robert Pougheon, André Lhote, René Buthaud and Jean Despujols. Although their monumental and allegorical paintings of women tended towards the neo-classical, they were wholly of the period in terms of drawing and colours, as well as in such specific details as stylized flowers, make-up, hairstyle and costume.

The female figures of René Buthaud often adorned Art Deco ceramics, and were executed not only on stoneware but also on frescoes and in watercolours. AndrE Lhote, who was the teacher of Tamara de Lempicka, was himself self-taught and achieved landscapes, genre scenes and figural works which were less caricatured and somehow both more geometric and spiritual than the works of the other painters.

One of the most popular Art Deco artists, especially in the United States, was the French-born Louis Icart, whose coloured etchings and aquatints perfectly captured the image of the chic, attractive, sometimes slightly risqué woman of the 1930s, part-Hollywood poster girl, part-Parisian fashionplate. She reclined in a gossamer gown; her hair was usually marcelled, her high-arched brows pencil-thin, her eyes heavily shadowed, and her lips a reddened Cupid's bow. She was often smoking and accompanied by a greyhound, poodle or borzoi.

German, Austrian, Scandinavian and American painters also created works that can loosely be termed Art Deco, especially their stylized portraits of chic or androgynous women. The Paris-based American Romaine Brooks, for instance, depicted Una, Lady Troubridge, in a dapper man's suit and short hair, complete with monocle and a pair of dachshunds, while the Danish-born Gerda Wegener painted sensuous female nudes in erotic poses, but in distinctly modern settings.

Although American artists such as Stuart Davis, Georgia O'Keeffe, Rockwell Kent and Joseph Stella produced works in the Machine Age idiom, celebrating industry, progress and big-city architecture, the vigorous Art Deco painting that thrived in

*The exotic urban landscape, above, a 1926 design for a backcloth by Russian artist Natalia Gontcharova; it was for the Ballets Russes production danced to Stravinsky's Oiseau de Feu (Firebird). Gontcharova frequently worked for Sergei Diaghilev, designing both costumes and stage sets for his ballets. She was largely influenced by religious art and folk tradition, as the multitiered `skyline' of onion domes on this drawing shows.*

France did not on the whole influence American artists, except perhaps in the occasional allegorical mural that embellished a movie-theatre lobby.

Sculpture in the Art Deco style was considerably more widespread than painting, especially in the variations on and imitations of the small decorative figures made mostly in Germany of ivory and cold-painted bronze, sometimes termed "chryselephantine". Ivory carving dates back to pre-biblical times, and by the eighteenth century the town of Erbach in Hesse had become its European centre. The greatest chryselephantine sculptor of the Art Deco period, Ferdinand Preiss, was a native of Erbach and descended from carvers on both sides of his family. In 1906, he moved to Berlin to found a workshop with Arthur Kassler, whose trademark, P.K., became world famous. Preiss's figures were beautifully executed

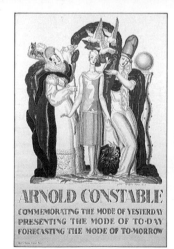

*exandre Kéléty's bronze group of alking panthers, below, is both otic and sensuous. Kéléty was a ungarian-born sculptor who worked Paris, often producing ryselephantine figures of female bjects. This feline group is a unning departure from those atues.*

*ench painter Jean Dupas designed e 1928 poster, right, for New York's nold Constable. Known for his eet-faced, lavishly clad, elongated males, Dupas also designed for ndon Transport, and was sponsible for the huge history of vigation mural in glass on the liner ormandie.*

*he silver-embellished watercolour, r right, is called Pearls, and hings and Palm Beach (The reakers). It is by Emil J. Bisttram, a ungarian emigré to the US who orked in advertising, and also inted – first realistic seascapes, en moderne images such as this, d later, more abstract works.*

statuettes, usually female, often dressed in exotic costumes and leaping about energetically on elaborate marble or onyx bases. Their facial features were painted on to the ivory (in the manner of classical Greek polychrome) which had first been carved by hand and then polished. The cast-bronze sections were also painted or otherwise embellished, and the finished pieces, although designed to be merely decorative, and in part mass-produced, were none the less miniature masterpieces and are today much sought after.

Most of the skipping, dancing statuettes were rather innocuous and innocent, but one artist, Bruno Zach, created erotic women – often leather-clad, whip-wielding, cigarette-smoking and topless – which bordered on the perverted.

Other sculptors worked in bronze or stone alone, such as Maurice Guiraud Rivière, the brothers Jan and Joël Martel and François Pompon. Unlike the decorative ivory and bronze figures of Preiss *et al*, the works of these and other sculptors could usually be safely termed sculpture and not decoration, whether they were representational or abstract. The Martels and Pompon created animal sculptures which were sleek and highly stylized, even angular, constructions. Guiraud Rivière's figures – like those of Paul Manship, Boris Lovet-Lorski, William Zorach and Carl Paul Jennewein in the United States – were massive, often allegorical figures, sometimes cast as outdoor architectural elements, sometimes as small indoor sculptures. Their forms were essentially neo-classical, quite unlike those of the truly avant-garde Jean Lambert-Rucki (influenced by totemic African art); the Britons Eric Gill and John Duncan Fergusson; Josef Csaky, Alexander Archipenko, Gustave Miklos, Jacob Epstein, Jacques Lipchitz, Raymond Duchamp-Villon, and of course the Rumanian-born Constantin Brancusi, whose sleek simplified abstract forms were inspired by African sculptures, but imbued with a strong sense of Machine Age modernism.

Gaston Lachaise's sculptures celebrated woman as a powerful, heroic Venus, not unlike Cycladic images of goddesses with unnaturally large breasts, thighs and bellies. Fellow American Elie Nadelman's sculptures could be classical bronzes – such as the gentle, monumental *Resting Stag* of c.1917 – or they could be humorous, painted-wood vignettes, like the dancing couple of *Tango* and the smiling *Woman at the Piano*, both of around the same time. John Storrs was perhaps the most eclectic American Art Deco sculptor of all: his monumental *Ceres* presents a strong, Cubist-inspired allegorical vision, whereas *New York* and *Forms in Space* (both c.1924–25) are strong architectonic abstractions. Planes and volume were Storrs' main considerations, and his various creations, whether figural or abstract, clearly show this.

The ivory and bronze bust, right, is of the chryselephantine type popular in the Art Deco era. The woman wears an elaborately decorated cloche hat, with black and gold triangles adorning the centre of the cap, as well as the draped collar. This anonymously created bust is unusual for such sculptures, which tended to be full length.

The Valkyrie maiden on horseback, above, is entitled Towards the Unknown. Belgian-born Claire-Jeanne-Roberte Colinet was its sculptor. Her works varied from traditional dancing figures to romantic equestrienne images.

Ferdinand Preiss created the magnificent Flame Leaper, right. Kinetic sculptures like this are the most interesting of chryselephantine works, and Preiss's were some of the most beautiful and energetic.

Paul Philippe created the Group of Dancers in ivory and cold painted bronze, below. The lithe, lively women sport short, wavy hairstyles in the garçonne mode, but their bodies, clad in form-revealing gowns, are anything but boyish. Philippe's sculptures are usually more elegant, attenuated and moderne than those of most of his contemporaries, which often tend to the theatrical, garish or sentimental.

The serene ivory face of Gerdago's harlequin dancer, right, is nearly lost in all her sartorial splendour. Gerdago's dancing figures often were clad in elaborate, exotic costumes and head dresses, many of which were polychromed and then finished with lacquer.

One of the great chryselphantine sculptors was Rumanian-born Demêtre Chiparus, who worked in Paris. His charming Pierrot and Pierrette, above, were inspired by the Ballets Russes, like many of his works.

A popular printmaker of the Art Deco period was Louis Icart, whose 1926 drypoint and etching, Fumée (Smoke), appears below. His blatantly erotic females were often surrounded by fur – either in the guise of a sleek canine companion or, as here, a lavish bed covering.

La Naissance d'Aphrodite, or The Birth of Venus, was depicted in a Cubist manner by Paul Véra in the 1925 oil-on-canvas, right. Véra was a versatile painter, wood-engraver, sculptor and fabric designer. The ornate frame, like so many surrounds for modern art, seems incongruous.

The c.1934 ivory sculpture, below, is by Emile Just Bachelet. Called Venus et l'Amour, the erotic pair was carved from an elephant tusk over 4ft (124cm).

The mask-like carved alabaster head, right, by Georges Coste, has a somewhat spiritual quality. The high arched brows and almond-shaped eyes of the androgynous face are also vaguely Egyptian. The sparse noodle-like curls, however, make a strange hairstyle for this mysterious creature.

The lovely illustration, far right, by John Austen adorned the frontispiece of a 1928 limited edition of 500 of Manon Lescaut. Austen was a British graphic artist and illustrator who was said to have "infuse[d] the spirit of the text" into his drawings. Notice the similarities between this woman's features, especially her eyes and brows, and those of the sculpture to her left. Such stylizations were associated with an ideal female image of the 1920s and 30s.

## TAMARA DE LEMPICKA

Tamara de Lempicka (1898–1980) was a Warsaw-born beauty whose whirlwind social life and distinctive portraits reflected the glittering aspect of the Art Deco era and style. De Lempicka studied painting in Russia, but in 1918 fled to Paris with her husband, Tadeusz Lempicki, whom she had helped to set free from imprisonment by the Bolsheviks. In Paris, De Lempicka studied painting with Maurice Denis and André Lhote, and thereafter proceeded to paint the portraits of other Eastern European refugees (mostly of royal lineage), famous writers, successful businessmen, fellow artists and her family (she had one daughter, Kizette). Her dramatic, vividly hued portraits were often sensuous and suggestive,

sometimes surreal or frightening. Especially memorable are those with strong backgrounds, be they architectural or floral settings, or billowy folds of fabric, or a line of ships' prows, as on the portrait, above. For some of her paintings she used anonymous models, either singly, in erotic pairs or in groups, nude or clothed, full-figure or facial. With the threat of war, De Lempicka, now remarried to the Hungarian Baron Raoul Kuffner, fled for the United States, where she painted Hollywood moguls and screen stars, as well as notable New Yorkers. One critic deemed de Lempicka "the perverse Ingres of the Machine Age", but without a doubt she was the most successful – and glamorous, with her

Garboesque looks – portrait artist of the period. Since the early 1970s, in the wake of a Tamara De Lempicka retrospective in Paris and renewed interest in Art Deco in general, her works have been appreciated not only for capturing on canvas the inhabitants of an opulent era in a rich, telling manner, but also for their sublime painterly qualities – such as on the melancholy, moving *Lady in Blue* of 1939, in the Metropolitan Museum of Art. De Lempicka painted for most of her life, but the work between 1924 and 1939, while in Paris, distinguishes her above all other Art Deco painters.

*Tamara de Lempicka, the Polish-born painter who lived in Paris in the 1920s and 30s, painted* Portrait of Arlette Boucard, *above, in 1928. This is one of some hundred distinctive pictures De Lempicka painted for rich, royal and socially connected clients. It is a sensuous depiction of the daughter of a scientist named Dr Boucard, who had become vastly wealthy by inventing the medicine Bacteol, the name written on the prow of one of the ships in the harbour background of the painting. De Lempicka also painted portraits of Dr and Mme Boucard.*

The watercolour above is by André Edouard Marty, whose illustrations often appeared in La Gazette du Bon Ton. Although a design for an interior, the 1939 drawing captures a loving moment between a stylishly gowned Parisienne and her child. Marty also enamelled jewellery and other pieces for Camille Fauré's workshop at Limoges.

The oil-on-card painting Flamant Rose (Pink Flamingo) right, was painted by Raphael Delorme. He was noted for his bulky female nudes, most of whom he situated in strange architectural settings. The vase-bearing woman here is seen amid a variety of Cubist motifs, with the title subject open-winged behind her.

The oil-on-canvas, left, depicts a couple from French pantomime, Pierrot et Columbine. *The 1921 painting is by Irene Lagut.*

Best known for his large outdoor sculptures, Briton Charles Sargeant Jagger created the handsome portrait of a casual but confident HRH, The Prince of Wales, right, in 1922.

Japanese-born Tsuguharu Foujita lived for a short time in London before settling in Paris, where he painted the picture above in 1917. Most of his art combined traditional oriental techniques with Western subjects, although this figure with bird is wholly Eastern in flavour. Foujita also produced etchings and lithographs.

Besides his many lacquered objects, the versatile Jean Dunand produced some lovely mixed-media flat works, such as the Portrait of Louise Boulanger, right, of watercolour, charcoal, pastel, and gold and silver paint. The subject's face shines, even above her brightly patterned shawl.

In 1932 Constantin Brancusi created the polished bronze, right, Jeune Fille Sophistiquée. *The Rumanian-born sculptor moved to Paris in 1904, where he produced abstract forms, usually comprising one or several ovoid or cylindrical shapes. Simplicity and purity were paramount to Brancusi, who abhorred realism.*

The jaunty dancer, below, is by Jan and Joël Martel, *twin brothers who sculpted in a variety of materials. Best known for their animal carvings, the Martels also created Cubist abstractions and human figures – such as this 1925 piece inspired by a Swedish ballet dancer.*

Above is Le Joueur de Scie Musicale (Musical Saw Player), *by Jan and Joël Martel, inspired by the musician Gaston Wiener. Comprising sheets of* zinc, the 1927 sculpture is markedly different from the twins' colourful dancer, left. At the 1925 Paris Exposition, the brothers created concrete Cubist trees for the garden of their friend Robert Mallet-Stevens, who later designed Martel House for them in Paris.

The premier figurative sculptor in America was Paul Manship, whose bronze Prometheus fountain, left, enhances New York's Rockefeller Center. Manship travelled and studied in Italy and Greece, and his love of antique art is evident in his work. The Rockefeller Center also used the sculptural talents of Lee Lawrie.

Russian sculptor Alexander Archipenko, who created The Metal Lady, below, in 1923, exhibited at the Paris salons from 1910. In the 1920s he settled in the US, participating in exhibitions, designing display windows for New York department stores and continuing to create abstract, Cubist sculptures in various metals, either relief or three-dimensional.

In 1909 Gustave Miklos moved to Paris from Budapest. He designed carpets and metalwork for couturier Jacques Doucet, for whom he sculpted the rock-crystal objet, below; right, his Tour Architecturale (Architectural Tower) of 1924.

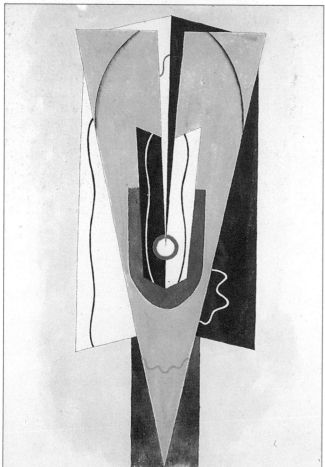

Jean Lurçat, whose 1922 still life is shown, top, started out as a Cubist painter, but turned to tapestry design by the 1930s, working for Aubusson and Gobelins, among others. Both the colours and subject of the painting pre-figure future tapestry designs of Lurçat's.

Better known for his Cubist sculpture, the Hungarian-born Joseph Csaky created Abstraction, in 1922. From 1908 Csaky lived in Paris, where he exhibited with the Cubists. The colourful drawing, which depicts an abstract face, is most likely a study for a three-dimensional work.

The gilt-bronze head, right, is by Pablo Gargallo and is a portrait of Kiki de Montparnasse. Despite its obvious abstract qualities, the smartly coiffed and (partially) made-up head is very much of the Art Deco era. It dates from 1928.

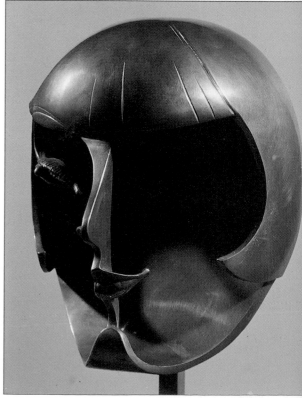

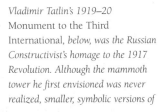

Vladimir Tatlin's 1919–20 Monument to the Third International, *below, was the Russian Constructivist's homage to the 1917 Revolution. Although the mammoth tower he first envisioned was never realized, smaller, symbolic versions of* the skewed spiral, such as the one shown, were. Tatlin believed in a strong connection between design and engineering, developing an aesthetic based on standardization, construction and mass-production.

New York, *the c.1925 bronze left, is by John Storrs, the Chicago-born, Europe-educated sculptor known for his stunning non-representational work.*

Jean Lambert-Rucki *painted the above oil-on-board* Montmartre *in 1925. Born in Poland, Lambert-Rucki collaborated with Dunand, Le Corbusier and Mallet-Stevens, among others, but he is best known for his own lacquered-wood, totemic sculptures.*

## JOHN STORRS

The greatest sculptor of the Art Deco style in the United States was John Storrs (1885–1956), who studied and worked extensively abroad, including a stint in 1914 at the studio of Auguste Rodin. His sculpting career spanned both sides of the Atlantic, where he showed his distinctive, non-representational work to great acclaim in Paris and New York. His father was an architect and speculative builder, so it is not surprising that many of Storrs' greatest creations showed a strong architectonic quality. But although his tall, stepped, metal pieces resembled structures, they were first and foremost complex modern essays in planes and volumes, and in shadow and light. Some of his creations were all-bronze, such as *New York*, illustrated to the left, while others were mixed-media sculptures which utilized aluminium, brass, copper, wood and other materials. Storrs executed figurative works as well, such as the Machine-Age *Ceres*, cast in chromium-plated steel and now on top of the Chicago Board of Trade building.

Storrs was principally recognized as a fine sculptor, although his interests in architecture, as well as industrial design, make him an outstanding figure in the Art Deco era. His work is included in such renowned collections as those of the Whitney Museum of American Art in New York and the Musée National d'Art Moderne at the Centre Georges Pompidou in Paris.

Zephyr *digital clock by Kem Weber, for Lawson Time Inc, brass and copper, c.1933.*

# CHAPTER • NINE

## INDUSTRIAL

# DESIGN

Together with the skyscraper and the architectural off-shoots that took root in America in the 1930s, another type of design with far-reaching implications burgeoned west of the Atlantic – industrial design. The industrial revolution had long since taken place, the Machine Age was flourishing, and the design of handsome domestic objects, large and small, static and kinetic, was an inevitable outcome. Industrial designers in the United States did not, in the main, develop their products along the lines of the great French *objets*; this was partly because the depression that followed the Wall Street crash of 1929 imposed financial restraints. The Bauhaus school, however, was strongly influential on these designers, many of whom had emigrated from Europe.

They were talented and innovative, creating mass-produced wares which, as one expert has written, were "sleekly formulated to evoke French chic", but were nevertheless as American as high-style Art Deco was French. American industrial design has been called the streamlined style, Art Moderne, or Modernism; but whatever its name, it transformed the look of American, and subsequently of European, households, offices, schools and landscapes. With its shiny surfaces, new materials, shapes largely adapted from industrial forms (the streamlined ones firmly founded on aerodynamic principles), it fully expressed the newly invented word "beautility". By the late 1920s, with consumer products proliferating and competition rampant, marketing became essential, and the look of a product often took priority over its performance.

The imaginative minds associated with this Modernist movement in America – Raymond Loewy, Walter Dorwin Teague, Norman Bel Geddes, Russel Wright, Walter von Nessen, Donald Deskey, Henry Dreyfuss, Gilbert Rohde, Kem Weber among them – designed everything from cigarette lighters, cameras, toasters and vacuum cleaners, to furniture, cars, trains and aeroplanes. They "restyled" fairly new appliances such as electric lamps, fans, fires, refrigerators and radios, and 'revolutionized' objects that had been in use for centuries – clocks, teapots and scales, for example.

The vocabulary of the industrial designer was primarily that of industry, and the byword was "streamlining" – that is, smoothing away the bumps and angles to produce a bullet- or teardrop-shape, which offered the least resistance in terms of physics. The materials used were metal, wood, glass, plastic and other new or improved ingredients, and the final products were glossy, chic and extremely *moderne*.

Many of the designers had trained as engineers, so their mechanical approach to the expression of even the simplest object – for instance, a turned-metal powder compact with several tiny compartments, or a chrome-framed mantel clock – is obvious, as is their modern aesthetic sense. One of their exponents, Gilbert Rohde, wrote, "Industrial design is a very simple matter; it is design brought up to date, design in terms of a mass production economy instead of a handcraft economy." What was required, he continued, was "a modicum of art and

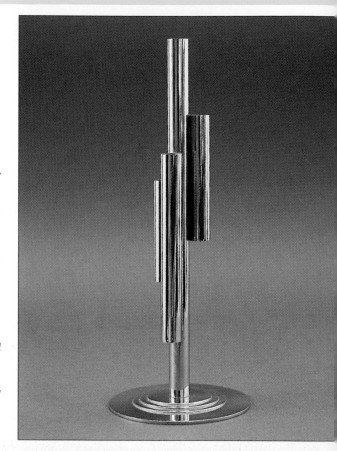

*The four-tubed bud vase of 1936, right, was mass-produced by Chase Brass & Copper Co of Connecticut. The vase shown is of polished chromium, but the model was also available in brass and copper. Chase was a pipe manufacturer which branched out into making small decorative objects, such as ashtrays, cocktail shakers, lamps, etc, in the 1930s.*

*The Bakelite bookends, below, sport a creamy green-and-yellow mottling and off-centre elliptical shapes which seem very* moderne *and streamlined for their c. 1920 date. They were made by J. Dickinson & Co, UK, under the trade name* Carvacraft.

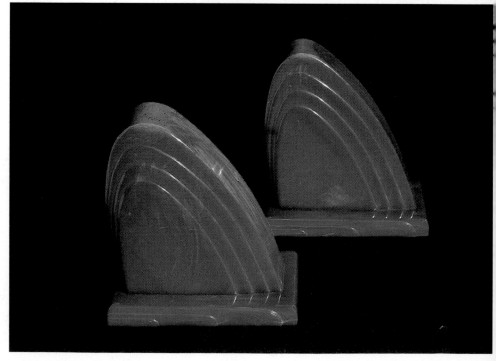

# INDUSTRIAL DESIGN

*...e plastic salt-and-pepper shakers, ...ght, are souvenirs of 1939 New ...rk's World's Fair. Cheap plastic ...jects such as these proliferated in ...e United States in the 1930s. Blue ...d orange were the official Fair ...ours, and the Trylon and ...risphere its architectural emblem.*

*...e powder compacts, above, are two ...amples of the many thousands ...ich were mass-produced in the US ...d Europe during the Art Deco ...riod. On the left is a handsome ...llow-metal and red-leather-like ...mpact by Elgin American; the ...astic square on the right is probably ...ench.*

"Kandem" lamp of Bauhaus designer Marianne Brandt, which, although it dates back to 1928, is a design classic, still much imitated today. The Chase Brass & Copper Co. of Waterbury, Connecticut, produced ornamental pieces whose basic ingredients – pipe, sheet metal, chromium – had been the mainstay of the firm's earlier, entirely functional, output. Walter von Nessen designed a sleek cake and sandwich trowel for them, and the illustrator Rockwell Kent produced both an ice bucket and a wine-bottle stand featuring a medallion of a grape-bearing infant Bacchus, but the majority of their distinctive new products were anonymously designed. These include a four-tube bud vase, available in either polished chromium or brass and copper; the "Blue Moon" cocktail shaker with matching cups made of chromium, blue glass and plastic; a globe-shaped ash receiver, and the "Airalite" vest-pocket flashlight (or torch), which resembled a rectangular powder compact or cigarette case.

The vacuum cleaner, or Hoover, an invention of the early twentieth century, had been an efficient but unattractive appliance with bulging visible motors, until industrial design came along. By the 1930s the works had all but disappeared under handsome bodies, largely due to Henry Dreyfuss, who preferred the term "cleanlining" to "streamlining", and applied his skills also to the cradle desk telephone for the Bell Telephone Company in 1937, the Toperator washing machine for Sears, Roebuck in 1933, and the Twentieth Century Ltd express train for New York Central in 1938.

Washing machines, refrigerators and other major appliances were also designed by Raymond Loewy, the French-born commercial artist whose first major commission, in 1929, was to modernize the Gestetner mimeograph machine. His best-known "face-lifting", however, was a sleek white-enamelled refrigerator with shiny chrome hardware, the Coldspot "Super Six" of 1935, for Sears, Roebuck, which started a new design trend in refrigerators.

The Machine Age brought with it more time for leisure activities, and industrial designers enthusiastically turned to items associated with hobbies and recreation. Walter Dorwin Teague, who designed objects as disparate as X-ray equipment and Texaco service stations, worked hand in hand with company engineers at Eastman Kodak to produce elegant and efficient cameras. Among these was his 1936 'Bantam Special', its compact, black-enamelled case highlighted with shiny horizontal lines which were not only pleasing to the eye, but were also practical; being slightly raised, they helped to prevent chipping or cracking of the lacquered surface. Teague's radios, or wireless sets, included a stunning case for Spartan in metal, wood and blue glass, which sat on sledge-like runners.

Gordon Russell and Betty Joel, both British, also designed radio cabinets, but most of the glass and Bakelite models which are so collectible today – one side usually rounded, the other straight-edged – were anonymous creations for Philco, Telefunken, RCA Victor, Emerson and other companies. Not all

engineering abilities". Commercial and graphic artists soon entered the field, their talented draughtsmanship often belying their lack of mechanical knowledge and engineering skills, and their designs, as a result, frequently working better on paper than in the home, the office or on the highway.

The 1930s saw the advent of the age of consumerism, with portable objects among the first to be 'transformed' by industrial designers; irons, staplers, pencil sharpeners, tape dispensers, tabletop and desk lamps, kitchen and factory tools, drinking glasses and vases were all faithfully produced along the lines of the new industrial-design creed. The Hotchkiss stapler of 1936, designed by Orlo Heller, was a typical example, with a handsomely styled off-centre parabolic form and a sleek-metal surface. Equally *moderne* were the Ronson company's similarly shaped table lighter in enamelled brass and the bedside radios, however, were sexily curved; the "Air King" model designed in about 1934 by Harold van Doren and John Gordon Rideout was a red plastic stepped pyramid which is far more skyscraper than streamlined bullet. The jukebox also made its debut in the 1930s, and although its heyday was not until the 1940s and '50s, its form was definitely of the period, often covered in shiny chrome, brightly coloured glass and vivid plastic in clearly stated Art Deco configurations.

Streamlining principles were, logically, best applied to objects that moved – automobiles, trains, aeroplanes, boats, trailers. Many of the designers who worked on small objects, among them Dreyfuss, Loewy and Norman Bel Geddes, also turned their talents to vehicles, and the results, although not always successful with the conservative consumer, were innovative and dramatic.

*The detail of the Philadelphia diner, above, with its shiny, yellow-banded corner looking like a layered birthday cake, took the materials and forms of industrial design and magnified them to architectural proportions. Even huge skyscrapers like the Chrysler and McGraw-Hill buildings sported jaunty stripes in shiny metal, polychromed terracotta and other materials.*

*...merson, the US firm, produced the ...dio, above, in the 1930s. The bright ...d Bakelite body is typical of ...merican radios of the time, which ...ere cheerier and more colourful ...an their British counterparts. The ...evelopment of more compact ...ectronic components allowed ...aller radio bodies (which were also ...all enough to be moulded from ...astic).*

*...he most luxuriant ocean-going vessel ... the French Line, the Normandie, is ...en against Manhattan's skyline on ...e cover of a vintage brochure, left; ...e artist's signature, 'Wilquin', ...ppears under the Statue of Liberty, ...ft. Although its exterior design was ...uite traditional, the Normandie's ...teriors, furniture and assorted ...bjects were designed by France's top ...ames.*

design of trains. The German State Railways' three-car diesel train of 1937 was torpedo-shaped, air-conditioned, could carry 100 passengers comfortably, and, most important, was speedy as well. Streamlined railcars were also used in France, where Italian Ettore Bugatti designed a car for the state railways in about 1934. In the United States, one engine was a Raymond Loewy design, and in Britain the 1935 "Mallard" locomotive, designed by Sir Nigel Gresley for the London and North Eastern Railway, was not only a strong and sleek essay in streamlining, but it set a world speed record for steam locomotives in 1938, travelling at 126 mph.

Aircraft, of course, benefited immeasurably from aerodynamic forms. The Boeing 247 of 1933 was the first commercial plane designed along these lines, soon followed by the Douglas DC1, DC2 and DC3, all of which had all-metal bodies, wing and fuselage integrations and stressed skins of light weight aluminium. The DC3 of 1935, which is said to have revolutionized air transport and been a work of art as well, was manufactured an amazing 13,000 times.

Although aluminium, chromium, stainless steel and other metal hybrids struck the keynotes of the streamlined era, it was another, far humbler material, synthetic plastic, that brought commercial mass-production up to date in a way no one could have imagined in previous decades. It had been introduced early in the twentieth century, but its usage became widespread only in the 1920s and 30s. Today, in its myriad forms and formulae, it has become a part of everyone's life, in our kitchen utensils, jewellery and boudoir accessories, our lamps, radios, television sets and even furniture.

Some streamlined objects have remained in production for many years, or are experiencing a comeback of sorts – for instance, the chromed-metal cocktail shakers of Chase and other manufacturers. On the whole, though, the era was short-lived but exciting, and its glorious postscript (some say apotheosis) was the 1939 World's Fair in New York, which highlighted the "World of Tomorrow". Its symbol, the simple but dramatic trylon and perisphere, represented limitless flight and controlled stasis. The exhibition's futuristic displays and pavilions in effect marked the end of the beginning of modernism, a period which had opened with the 1925 Exposition in Paris.

By the 1930s, most cars were streamlined, sometimes with only a subtle, barely discernible touch, such as on the Ford "V8" of 1933, with its gentle body 'parabolizing' over the front wheels; sometimes the statement was stronger, as in the Lincoln "Zephyr" of 1936, whose entire backside was one long uninterrupted curve. The futuristic, three-wheeled "Dymaxion" cars (1933–34) of the visionary R. Buckminster Fuller pulled out all the stops with their extreme teardrop shapes, which, however, proved far too radical for popular American taste and never even reached mass-production stage.

Trucks and buses too were streamlined; among the most striking were Raymond Loewy's designs for Grey-hound, for whom he also created graphics and coach-depot designs. Cosmetic streamlining was also applied to the many roadside diners which made their appearance in the United States in the 1930s and '40s, a result of the nation's increasing mobility, even a streamlined tractor made its appearance, produced by the Bohn Aluminum & Brass Corporation of Detroit. Its tenure was brief, however, unlike that of the "Airstream" trailer, which can still be seen on the roads today, a gleaming icon of an era past.

Streamlining was perhaps most successfully used in the

# CONSUMERISM

Christian Barman designed the enamelled-metal electric iron, below, for HMV. The 1934 design was one of several Barman produced for the British firm. The integration of handle with body results in a streamlined yet somewhat inchoate shape.

The Ingersoll alarm clock, right, has a case of cream-coloured urea, or urea formaldehyde, a type of amino plastic which is made from ammonia-based compounds. The stepped-pyramid design is adapted from architectural shapes, notably the huge stone temples of the Aztec and Mayan civilizations. The smart little clock was made in the United Kingdom.

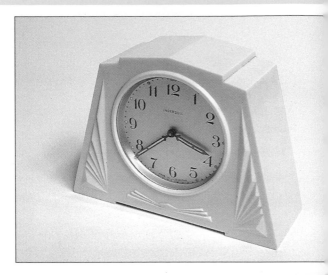

The 1923 Model 25 vacuum cleaner, above, was made by the Swedish-based firm, Electrolux Ltd, which in 1915 had perfected this type of compact horizontal-cylinder sweeper with flexible hose attachment. Because of this advance, upright-cleaner makers were compelled to produce similar attachments, so that items such as drapes and upholstery could also be cleaned.

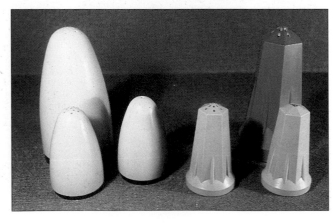

The two condiment sets, left, were made for Woolworth's by Streetly Manufacturing which was the biggest plastic-moulding company in the UK in the 1930s. Streetly was the first British firm to produce light-coloured, lightweight plastics ideal for domestic use.

The CWS hair dryer, above, dates from 1937. Its body is of urea plastic, its handle is phenolic. The L-shaped design is a classic one for hair dryers and similar models are still much in use today.

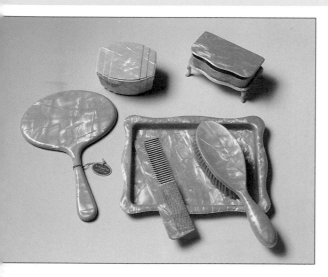

The 1930s dressing table set, left, is made of Xylonite, a cellulose-nitrate plastic which was marketed by the British David Spill Co (later the Xylonite Co). The shimmery pattern on the plastic attempted to replicate the veining of marble. The set's design is rather traditional, but for the stepped box at the top left.

Versatile industrial designer Raymond Loewy created the Electrolux refrigerator, right, in the late 1930s. It echoed the basic concept of his revolutionary Coldspot model for Sears, Roebuck in 1935 – that is, the whole encased in a sleek, white-enamelled box on low legs – but its angles and hardware were less prominent and geometric.

## RAYMOND LOEWY

Raymond Loewy (born in 1893) was arguably the most famous industrial designer in America in the Art Deco era. A native of France, Loewy had studied engineering there before emigrating to the United States in 1919. He started out as a fashion illustrator for *Vogue* magazine, then about a decade later he directed his myriad talents towards industrial design, his first commission being the redesign of Sigmund Gestetner's Duplicator.

Subsequent commissions came fast and furiously – for big and small domestic and consumer appliances (among them a pencil sharpener, radio and refrigerator); for all types of vehicles (automobiles, buses, locomotives, ferry boats); for shop-fittings, buildings and graphic designs, perhaps the best known of these being the bull's eye packaging for Lucky Strike cigarettes. Loewy is even credited with the near-iconic "Coca Cola" bottle, which had been developed in 1915 but was given a more distinctive shape by him some years later. At the peak of his success, the astute businessman employed hundreds of workers in American, British, French and Brazilian offices, and his clients numbered about 80. Something of a showman, Loewy was none the less foremost among American-based industrial designers.

he tray, right, is a simple design
ade of wood, metal and coloured
il. Such handsome geometric motifs
ppeared on the most everyday
usehold objects, evidence that the
fluence of high-style Parisian Art
eco filtered down even to ordinary
930s American kitchens, where this
ay would have been used.

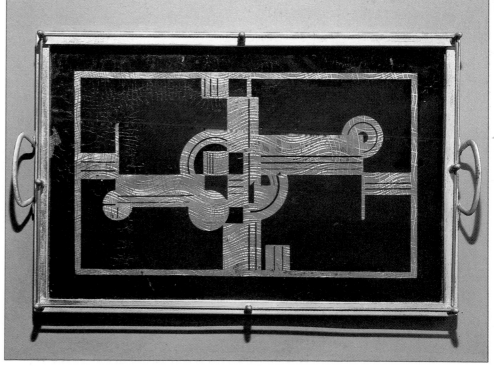

The Swedish telecommunication firm, L. M. Ericson, produced the three DB11 1001 table telephones below c.1932–37. The nicely proportioned, plastic-moulded model was designed by Jean Heiberg some six years before Henry Dreyfuss created his famous "300" desk set for Bell in the US.

The DBH 1001 had a universal appeal and was subsequently produced world-wide. The see-through model is especially interesting.

The 1939 Model 262 Hoover, shown in a promotional photograph on the right, sported a spaceship-like head, with a nattily striped bag to go with it.

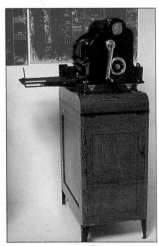

The plastic radio, box and camera, below, date from the 1930s. Their designs are rather old-fashioned, but their bodies represent a modern technological development.

Even such a mundane object as the electric fire was given a moderne look, as Wells Coates' 1934 model, above, for Isokon shows. Coates was a Canadian-born architect/industrial designer working in the UK.

The 1929 Gestetner Duplicator, above, may not look very streamlined, but Raymond Loewy's design – which he had only five days to produce – was none the less far more simplified than previous models.

Olivetti's MP1 typewriter, above was designed by Aldo Magnelli in 1932. The firm's founder, Camillo Olivetti, who designed its first typewriter in 1913, stated that a typewriter should be "serious and elegant"; MP1 is both, and compact as well.

The blue-enamelled metal container, right, depicting a sleek greyhound, is a US-made typewriter-ribbon box. The fact that such a sophisticated motif would adorn an everyday object such as this shows the extent of Art Deco's impact.

The hand-held fan, right, is made of tortoiseshell-like plastic. Whimsically called La Brise (The Breeze), the fan was made in England in the 1930s.

Red phenolic plastic makes up the body of the Coronet Midget 16mm still camera, left, from 1938. The Midget is compact and smartly designed, and the mottled plastic case adds a nice touch. The Coronet Camera Co was in Birmingham, England.

From the front, the cream-coloured Bakelite form barely reveals itself as a wireless. With its dials hidden at the back, the radio has a symmetrical and not at all technological look.

*Paquebot NORMANDIE de la C.ᵍᵉ Gᵉ Transatlantique.*
*Longueur 313.75 . Largeur 36ᵐ30 . Puissance 160.000cv.*
*Vitesse 30 nœuds, soit : 54 km. heure. Jauge 75.000 tonnes.*
*Passagers 3500.*

Although its exterior design was quite conventional, the French ocean liner Normandie, shown left in a G. DuFresse watercolour, was a "floating palace" furnished with luxurious objets by the likes of Lalique, Puiforcat and Dunand. Launched in 1935, the ship sank in New York harbour in 1942.

The American industrial designer, Norman Bel Geddes, created the streamlined, tear-drop-shaped prototype for a bus, below, in 1939. Geddes began his career as an advertising artist and stage-set designer, and created the popular General Motors exhibit, "Highways and Horizons", at the 1939 New York World's Fair.

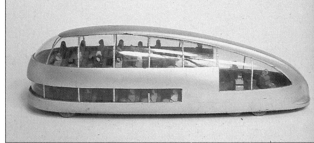

The smart, urea-plastic speedometer dial, right, featured in the 1936 model Talbot. The predominant oval shapes, against a ground of black cross-hatching, create a sleek overall design. It was designed by the British firm, Jaeger.

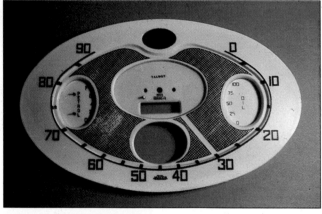

Ponderous, yet somehow elegant motor cars appeared in the 1930s, such as the Delahaye automobile featured in a c.1930 British publication, left. Note the many curves, even extending to the licence plate.

The Lincoln-Zephyr V-12, advertised in a 1937 issue of Punch, right, promised the driver "sheer, sensuous delight". The tear-drop shape arcs nicely over all four wheels.

Airplanes, too, were subjected to streamlining; the poster, left, gives an interesting overview of a 1930s British craft. The sleek body of the plane, seen from above, could almost be that of a moderne train.

At right is a colourful 1935 poster for The Silver Jubilee, touted as "Britain's First Streamline Train". Its designer was Sir Nigel Gresley, another of whose A4 steam locomotives set a 126mph (203 km/h) record in 1938.

A large internal-combustion engine powered the City of Salina M10000, below, Union Pacific's streamlined train which debuted in the mid-1930s. Its front end, studded with rivets, resembles a helmet.

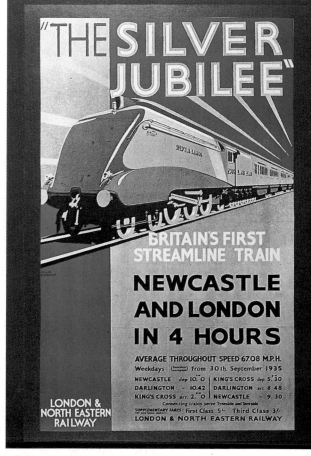

*Poster for 1925 Paris Exposition by Robert Bonfils, France*

# CHAPTER • TEN
# BOOKBINDING
# AND
# GRAPHICS

The basic stylization – the geometricization – of the Art Deco period lent itself well to graphics of all kinds, including posters, book and magazine illustrations, advertisements, packaging and the like. Even the fine art of bookbinding flourished, as it had done in the Art Nouveau era, with some of the top names in French design applying their talents to book covers – and sometimes using the same opulent materials as in their furniture and other designs.

The turn of the century in France witnessed a boom in bookbinding, with designers and craftsmen forsaking traditional motifs and techniques and producing innovative designs, very much in keeping with the naturalistic, curvilinear bent of the Art Nouveau style, which then predominated. By the 1920s, the Art Deco style, with its bright colours, geometric elements and sumptuous materials, had taken over. Morocco and calf leathers and gold and silver tooling remained staples of the binder's craft, but such lavish materials as sharkskin, mother-of-pearl, ivory, exotic woods, lacquer, snakeskin and *coquille d'oeuf* (crushed eggshell) began to be used as well, with the tooling sometimes in platinum or palladium. Although most of the premier Art Deco bookbindings included no lettering on their covers, some incorporated the titles effectively, using gilt *moderne* letters to complement the geometric motifs.

The designers included many whose work appeared in other mediums: Jean Dunand, the furniture designers – Rose Adler, André Mare and Pierre Legrain, the graphic artist Robert Bonfils and the Swiss-born François-Louis Schmied. Jean Dunand often executed lovely lacquer plaques for book covers, sometimes designed by Schmied, which included colourful landscapes, stylized floral motifs, abstract patterns and exotic figures and animals. One handsome example was a roundel illustrating a panther and a young man for Rudyard Kipling's *Jungle Book*, or *Le Livre de la Jungle*.

Pierre Legrain, who became the most influential designer of bindings in the 1920s, received his first major commission – from the couturier Jacques Doucet – with no experience whatsoever in the field; he had, however, previously designed jewellery, furniture and gowns. In a two-year period, he designed some 365 bindings for Doucet – one every other day – all of which were executed by professional binders. Rose Adler also designed bindings for Doucet, even more exotic than Legrain's and sometimes encrusted with precious stones. Her maroon morocco-leather binding for Colette's *Chéri* (1925) is stylish, with twelve metallic circles at the left giving way to a huge hemisphere at the right, which is actually the letter "C" enclosing the last four letters of the title.

Legrain rarely designed figural bindings, but others, notably Bonfils, did – usually sharply angled or modishly decorative silhouettes, seldom full-colour figures. Bonfils was himself also an executor of bindings, working with André Jeanne, a professional binder who also produced designs for Rose Adler and for such other gifted practitioners as Paul Bonet and the father-and-son team of Louis and Henri Creuzevault. Louis Creuzevault often created abstract or floral patterns, as well as covers with three-dimensional applications of differently coloured leathers. In 1930 he produced a binding for Georges Duhamel's *Scènes de la vie future* that was distinctly *moderne*.

François-Louis Schmied, a man of many talents, not only designed covers but also illustrated books; designed them and their typefaces; created their lettering; made wood engravings of illustrations for them, and even printed them on his own presses. His bindings ranged from subdued monochromatic enlivened only by gilt lettering to opulently multi-coloured, often set with lacquer panels, executed either by Dunand or by the Cubist-influenced designer Jean Goulden. A lovely Schmied binding for Paul Fort's *Les Ballades françaises* featured a green and silvered-metal plaque by Dunand showing stylized birds on a background of dots in a rainbow pattern.

Paul Bonet, a fashion designer turned bookbinder, was imaginative and innovative, with metallic bindings; cut-out bindings that revealed a design on the endpapers, and related but varying designs and lettering on the spines of works with more than one volume, such as on Marcel Proust's *A la Recherche du temps perdu*.

Some binders incorporated photographic elements in their covers, among them Laure Albin Guillot, who specialized in microphotography, enlarging minute biological specimens – plankton, for instance – to produce unusual, pseudo-abstract designs. Other of her bindings included human

*The somewhat angular celebrity portraits, above – including Churchill, Chaplin and Shaw – appear on Straight Line Caricatures, cigarette cards issued in 1926 by John Player & Sons. Such giveaway ephemera were highly collectable in the 1920s.*

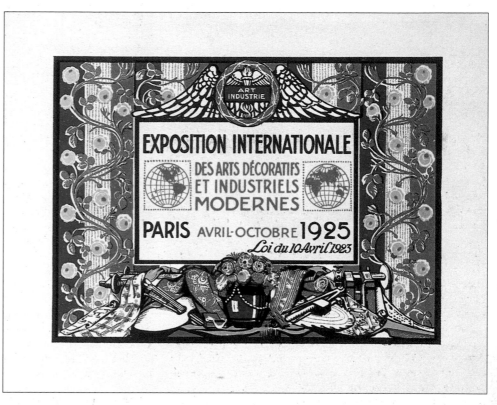

images, such as an erotic, back-posed nude on Pierre Loûys's *Les Chansons de Bilitis*.

In other western countries, the finest bookbinders adhered largely to traditional materials, methods and designs. However, mass-produced, printed covers in Germany, Britain, the United States and elsewhere often depicted Art Deco figures and motifs. The stylized lettering which came to be associated with 1920s Paris was also frequently seen. A 1932 English-language edition of Bruno Bürgel's *Oola-Boola's Wonder Book* displays such lettering – bold, in several sizes and decorated in blind stamping with simple vertical and horizontal bands.

In the United States, the Greek-born John Vassos and Ruth Vassos designed and produced bindings of note, often for their own coloured-cloth-on-board books, which included *Contempo* (1928), *Ultimo* (1930) and *Phobia* (1931). These catchy, contemporary titles appeared in thick bold lettering on grounds highlighted by equally bold geometric designs. Vassos was also known for his industrial designs.

Posters, graphics, decorative prints, advertisements, magazines, books and other printed matter – whether mass-produced giveaways or limited-edition works of art – proliferated in the 1920s and 1930s. The rise of modernism witnessed a growth of the printed word and picture as well,

presaging today's torrential out-pouring of the mass media. Printing methods, especially colour reproduction processes, had vastly improved in the nineteenth and early twentieth centuries, as had the quality of the finished product, encouraging top-ranking artists and illustrators to accept commissions.

Graphics had become bolder, broader, more geometric, less ornamented and, perhaps most important, highly legible. The first of the century's sans serif typefaces, "Railway", had been designed in 1918 by Edward Johnston, for the London Underground system. The Bauhaus typographer Herbert Bayer's "Universal" typeface introduced in 1925 was void not only of serifs and other decorative elements, but indeed even of capital letters! Even the Cyrillic alphabet took on strongly angular lines in the 1920s, in graphics by, among other, Vladimir Tatlin, El Lissitzky and Natalia Goncharova. In 1920s France, however, decorative touches were added to – rather than subtracted from – typefaces, a logical development, considering the vogue for decoration in every other medium. This was manifested primarily in the juxtaposition of thick and thin elements within a single letter, or in decorative shading that entirely eliminated a part of a letter. M. F. Benton's *Parisian* (1928) is an example of thick-thin characters, and A. M. Cassandre's *Bifur* (1929) consisted of letters that were nearly unrecognizable, except for their grey areas.

*The colour plate, above left, represents L'Océanie (Oceania), and was one of a series of exotic place images on a 1921 calendar designed by George Barbier.*

*Far-off places held great appeal for French designers in the 1920s.*

*Directly above is the cover of a 1923 pamphlet announcing the upcoming 1925 Paris Exposition. Although the floral motifs could loosely be identified as Art Deco, the overall, cluttered feel of the image harks back to an earlier era.*

THE SENSATIONAL HUNGARIAN SUICIDE SONG

*The French label, below, for a chocolate bar is awash with Art Deco motifs: concentric circles, arcs, stylized waves and typical typeface –* *bold and black-and-white but for the centre word, which is thick white and outlined with red zigzags.*

The motifs of many of the vividly coloured posters and graphics of the period were characterized by sheer energy and exuberance, in part the result of the new obsession with speed and travel that accompanied the fancy motor cars, fast trains and elegant ocean liners which were so much an expression of the 1920s and 1930s.

A. M. Cassandre (1901–1968), born Adolphe Mouron in Russia, was the outstanding poster artist and typographer of Art Deco Paris. His distinctive graphic style – bright colours combined with subtle shading, bold lettering often juxtaposed with wispy characters, and strong, angular, flat images – won him numerous awards. He is best known for his travel posters, the most famous among them, a streamlined, angled locomotive puffing decoratively for the *Nord Express* (1927) and a fiercely frontal view of the liner *Normandie* (1935). The posters of Jean Carlu, as well as of many others in France and elsewhere, were heavily inspired by Cassandre's work.

Paris' second most important poster designer was Paul Colin, whose often light-hearted illustrative style, although neither as austere nor as classy as Cassandre's, was equally effective. Originally the poster artist and stage designer for the Théâtre des Champs-Elysées, Colin's images include a memorable depiction of a saucy Josephine Baker with two black jazz musicians in a poster advertising *La Revue Nègre*. He depicted Miss Baker in several paintings as well, and also designed stunning posters advertising not only other performers but cigarettes and other products, nearly all of which featured human figures, sometimes highly stylized, sometimes lovingly caricatured.

Charles Gesmar, who is best remembered for his posters of the Casino de Paris performer Mistinguett, designed in a more curvilinear and ornate style, à la 1900. He usually used stark lettering, but occasionally became rather fanciful, with letters resembling those of Jean-Gabriel Domergue on his poster for the dancers Maarcya & Gunsett.

*The haunting black and white artwork on the sheet-music cover, is quite appropriate for the song annotated within – Gloomy Sunday (acclaimed at the upper right as "The Sensational Hungarian Suicide Song").*

*The dramatic and somewhat frightening bow of an unnamed French ship looms overhead in the stunning 1935 poster, right, by A. M. Cassandre (the same image was used to advertise the Normandie liner). The Russian-born Cassandre was France's best-known poster artist, as*

*well as a significant designer of typefaces. Alliance Graphique, the advertising agency which he co-founded with Maurice Moyrand, was extremely successful, with cigarette companies, newspapers, and railroad lines among its clients.*

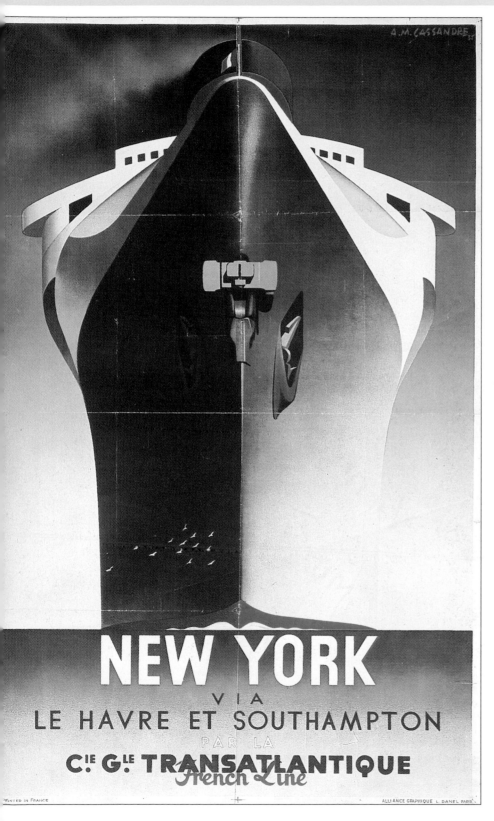

Three memorable posters were created for the 1925 Paris Exposition – by Charles Loupot, Robert Bonfils and Girard. Loupot's design cleverly juxtaposed industry and decoration, depicting a massive factory with wisps of black smoke cutting across clouds shaped like stylized flowers. Bonfils' image was totally decorative, featuring a stylized Greek maiden carrying a basket of stylized flowers, and accompanied by a dark leaping deer.

In Britain, the United States and Germany, most poster designs were pared down and geometric, using the bold rectilinear typefaces that were fast becoming the norm. Edward McKnight Kauffer, the American-born designer who also created rugs (see the section on carpets), worked both in England and in Hollywood, producing striking designs for, among others, the film *Metropolis*, Shell Petroleum and London Transport. While his London Transport posters tended to be quite Cubist and abstract, those of other designers were more colourful and representational, but always with easy-to-read typefaces. The French artist Jean Dupas designed a poster for LT, showing a scene of elegantly dressed ladies in Hyde Park.

Magazines of all sorts proliferated in the West in the 1920s and 1930s, the most influential in terms of graphics being those published in Paris. These included *Gazette du Bon Ton; Art, Goût, Beauté; Luxe de Paris; Vu* and *L'Illustration des Modes* (later *Le Jardin des Modes*). Their fashion and other illustrations, produced by such famous names as Georges Lepape, George Barbier, André Marty, Erté and Bernard Boutet de Monvel, had a great influence on design both in France and abroad.

Leading European and American magazines included the German *Styl, Harper's Bazaar, Femina, La Femme Chic, Pan, The New Yorker* and *Fortune. Vogue,* the most important fashion magazine of all, was always influential on both sides of the Atlantic, having begun publication in New York in 1892, in London in 1916 and in Paris in 1920.

The illustrations on the covers and inside pages of these publications portrayed not only outstanding general-interest and fashion images but also bold product "portraits". Great names in the design world contributed Raymond Loewy, Rockwell Kent, Joseph Binder, Ilonka Karasz and many others.

Floral designs flourished on advertisements and other Art Deco ephemera. Above, a display card for the floral scents of a French firm features bright cartoon blossoms on a black and gold ground.

Pale pastel shades are used to depict a simple, stylized blossom on the cover of this English card, whose inside text announced dance bands playing at London's Savoy Hotel. The half-shaded bifurcated design bears a resemblance to some contemporary typefaces.

Left, the floral motif on the Rose Vérité label is simplified.

The lush-looking label on the left, with its profusion of vivid geometric and floral motifs, was designed for a French liqueur bottle. Its colours and flora evoke an Egyptian setting.

The floral motif on the French powder box, left, is ultra-simplified, much as is the design on the Rose Vérité label at the bottom right of the opposite page. The bouquet is obviously in an architectural setting, yet a curious design element is the Pac-man-like white helmet enclosing the lower red blossom.

The eau-de-cologne label, left, is for the scent Pois de Senteur. Its English name noted parenthetically, Sweet Pea, leads one to believe that this product was intended for the British or American market. Note how much more realistic the blossoms are than those of the sign, also for the maker, Cheramy, at the far left.

Like the liquor label, Menthe, at the far left, the Rhum Vieux (Old Rum) image, right, is rich and inviting. Its palette is vivid, its design bold, and its message clear. Both labels, incidentally, have Jouneau, Paris, printed on them at the lower right. This may be the name of the artist, but it is more likely the signature of the printer.

# GEOMETRIC

HAUS BERGMANN „GOLD"

The pure geometry of the German cigarette box, left, for Haus Bergmann's Gold brand, carries over into the two smoking figures, stark black and white essays in the circle and the line.

The holiday booklet cover, right, from the English men's clothier, Austin Reed, manages to include the symbolic lion passant and a Yuletide tree. Both are presented in an angular yet seasonally colourful geometric context.

The opulent leather book-binding, right, made in Lyon, France, in 1936, covers Maurice Barrès' book, La Mort de Venise. It was bound by J. K. van West. The architectural form extending across the spine of the volume and creating a symmetrical design on the front and back covers was an unusual device begun in France in the 1920s. Before that, most bindings' decoration was limited to the front, with the back left plain. Note the silvery palladium highlighting the black tower, a metal inlay first used by Pierre Legrain, the most influential Art Deco bookbinder.

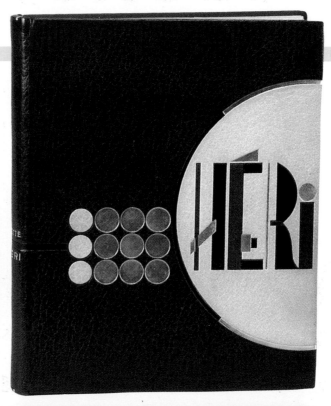

he English biscuit tin, below, sports a
unty black, red and gold geometric
esign which mimics the motifs on
more elaborate, less mundane objects.
The typeface, however, is not as
moderne as the design.

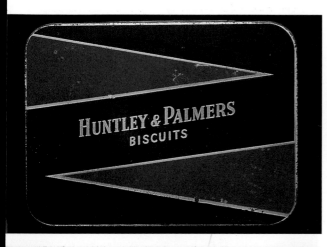

*Left, a stamped and foiled morocco
leather book-binding for Chéri, the
1920 classic by the celebrated French
novelist Colette. It was designed and
executed in 1925 by Rose Adler, a
talented Frenchwoman who produced
many bindings for the couturier-
collector Jacques Doucet. The
geometric elements of the binding are
dominated by the circle; especially
striking is the half-circle "C" enclosing
the four letters after it.*

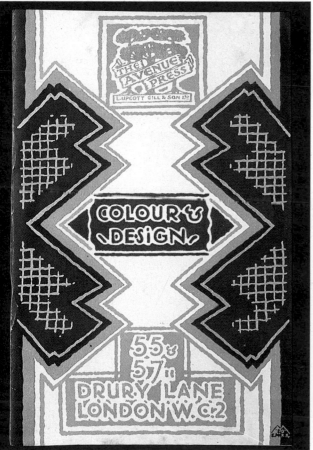

*The two designs on the left are
distinctive for both their geometric
elements and strong typefaces. The
book cover, far left, is English and was
created by Edward McKnight Kauffer,
a multi-talented, American-born
designer known also for his carpets;
the surface of the design has a
textural quality which is reminiscent
of that found on floor coverings. The
poster, left, is French, and has a
limited palette of red, black and gold,
appropriate to its white background
(Blanc, of course, means white). Note
the chequerboard pattern on the two
designs, both probably intended to
represent floor surfaces.*

# ILLUSTRATIVE FIGURES

L'Asie

L'Afrique

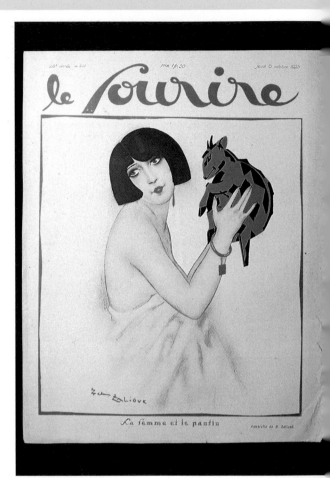

le sourire

La femme et le pantin

The two couples, above, were drawn in 1920 by George Barbier. The delicate ornament and costume of Asia were of great appeal to Art Deco designers, as was the lush exoticism of Africa.

S. Zaliouk designed the above right cover for La Sourire. The stylishly bobbed, scantily clad lady cluthes a cartoon beast reminiscent of the animal hybrids created by Jean Lambert-Rucki.

The illustrator known as Zig designed the 1930 poster, left, which features the incomparable Josephine Baker, plus feline admirer.

Even the most mundane products were fancily packaged by the 1930s, such as the British handkerchief box, right, covered with a golden-hued, quasi-oriental genre scene.

The 1925 poster of Casino de Paris performer Mistinguett, right, was created by Charles Gesmar, who attached himself to his subject at the age of 17, creating costumes, stage sets and posters for her act.

...helbert White painted this lively ...ene from the ballet Petrushka in ...026. The bright colours of the ...allets Russes' costumes and stage set ...ere a major influence on Art Deco ...aphic artists and couturiers.

...he costume design, right, for the ...aracter Assad in the ballet Dance ...e Jouet from A Thousand and ...ne Nights, is by Romain de Tirtoff, ...e Russian-born artist known as Erté ...rom the French pronunciation of his ...itials, RT). During his long career ...e worked for couturier Paul Poiret, ...s well as designing costumes and/or ...ts for the Folies Bergère, the ...iegfeld Follies and the Hollywood ...lm industry. His designs are highly ...ollectable today, and seemingly ...nlimited in number.

The 1931 Black & White whisky advertisement, above, features a masked harlequin and curtseying ballerina. Though not as opulent as French posters of the time, the theatrical quality of the British design is nevertheless apparent.

Paul Colin created some of the most exuberant figurative posters in 1920s Paris, such as the above image of Josephine Baker and two musicians (1925). A designer of stage sets as well as posters, Colin had a long association with the American-born singer-dancer, who captivated Parisian audiences with her exotic numbers for some 50 years.

A stylishly dressed couple poses on the paper fan, left, which would have been a giveaway advertising item. The amber and gold floral design framing the oval is typical of the period.

The jaunty caricature of French performer Maurice Chevalier, above, portrays him in his trademark straw hat, with pouting lower lip and black bow-tie beneath a tanned face. The image is not in any way intended to be an actual portrait, but it does capture the festive mood associated with the singing entertainer, who first achieved fame in Paris revues in the 1920s.

e French label, shows a dark-
red beauty in a garden of ferns.

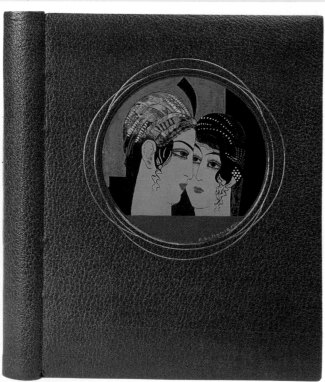

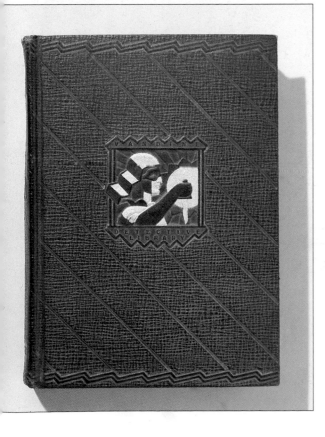

The stunning medallion attached to
the bookbinding, above, was designed
by François-Louis Schmied and
executed in exotic lacquer-work by
the talented and versatile Jean
Dunand. The red-leather binding
itself was done by Léon Gruel, who
began his career at the turn of the
century. Only 25 copies of the book,
Histoire Charmante de l'Adolescent
Sucré were made, each containing
illustrations hand-coloured by
Schmied, a Swiss graphic artist who
often collaborated with Dunand.

On the English book cover, left, is the
angular profile of a helmeted, dagger-
wielding masked man. The sinister
look is appropriate for the 1929
volume, one of a series of mystery
novels.

The German card above features the
comical caricatures of two hatted
gentlemen at the bottom, and the
seemingly incongruous profile of a
modish woman at top, complete with
scarlet-helmet hairstyle.

# TYPOGRAPHY

The lettering used in the 1920s and 1930s was a far cry from that used in the printed past. Thick, massive characters vied with thin, feminine ones, such as those seen on the British perfume advertisement, left, of 1937. The combination of different typefaces on one image was innovative for the time as well. The windswept hairstyle on the woman featured here is appropriate to the scent advertised, Sous le Vent (Under the Wind).

The smart, attenuated typeface on the travel poster, left, advertises the ocean liner Atlantis. Segregating the words to one corner of the page, and off centring the deckside scene, draws attention to both elemennt.

The dense characters comprising the lettering on the poster for the Chicago World's Fair of 1933, above, are in the same bold, upper-case typeface throughout. Note the patriotic colouring, the prominence of the androgynous winged head and the fading image of the native American in feathered headdress.